UNDERSTANDING ERICKSONIAN HYPNOTHERAPY

This book is a collection of selected writings by Dr. Sidney Rosen that aim to demystify the work of the leading psychiatrist, Dr. Milton Erickson, and illustrate Erickson's unconventional and life-changing hypnotic learning and strategic therapy.

An essential reading for those who seek to learn essential elements of psychotherapy, this collection elucidates fundamental aspects of Erickson's approaches and outlines factors effective in all forms of psychotherapy. It contains core teachings of many central elements in psychotherapy and stresses the importance of techniques such as therapeutic trance and hypnosis. As a student and close friend of Dr. Erickson, Dr. Rosen shares his own personal insights about Erickson's teaching methods in a direct and straightforward manner that allows readers easy access to Ericksonian philosophy and techniques.

Many therapists, both psychoanalytic and others, will find both Rosen's and Erickson's approaches compatible with their own and far removed from their preconceptions about hypnosis. Providing guidelines for providers of individual and group therapy, this book is an excellent guide to Ericksonian hypnotherapy.

Sidney Rosen, MD, is one of America's leading practitioners and teachers of Ericksonian Hypnotherapy. He is the editor of the bestselling book *My Voice Will Go With You: The Teaching Tales of Milton H. Erickson* (1982). The Founding President of the New York Milton H. Erickson Society for Hypnosis and Psychotherapy, Dr. Rosen practiced hypnotherapy in New York City for more than six decades.

Victor Kiarsis, LMSW, MBA, the editor of this collection, is a clinical therapist with a private practice in Rye, New York, and is a long-time student of Dr. Sidney Rosen.

UNDERSTANDING ERICKSONIAN HYPNOTHERAPY

Selected Writings of Sidney Rosen

Edited by Victor Kiarsis

With Foreword by Melvyn Bucholtz

First published 2020
by Routledge
52 Vanderbilt Avenue, New York, NY 10017

and by Routledge
2 Park Square, Milton Park, Abingdon, Oxon OX14 4RN

Routledge is an imprint of the Taylor & Francis Group, an informa business

© 2020 Sidney Rosen

The right of Victor Kiarsis to be identified as the author of the editorial material, and of Sidney Rosen for his individual chapters, has been asserted in accordance with sections 77 and 78 of the Copyright, Designs and Patents Act 1988.

All rights reserved. No part of this book may be reprinted or reproduced or utilised in any form or by any electronic, mechanical, or other means, now known or hereafter invented, including photocopying and recording, or in any information storage or retrieval system, without permission in writing from the publishers.

Trademark notice: Product or corporate names may be trademarks or registered trademarks, and are used only for identification and explanation without intent to infringe.

Library of Congress Cataloging-in-Publication Data
A catalog record for this title has been requested

ISBN: 978-0-367-26206-8 (hbk)
ISBN: 978-0-367-33884-8 (pbk)
ISBN: 978-0-429-32262-4 (ebk)

Typeset in Bembo
by Taylor & Francis Books

CONTENTS

Foreword	*vii*
Introduction	*xi*
Acknowledgements	*xiv*
Photos	*xv*
Original Article Publications	*xviii*

1	The Values and Philosophy of Milton H. Erickson	1
2	What Makes Ericksonian Therapy So Effective?	16
3	One Thousand Induction Techniques and Their Application to Therapy and Thinking	31
4	Concretizing of Symptoms and Their Manipulation	47
5	The Psychotherapeutic and Hypnotherapeutic Approaches of Milton H. Erickson, M.D.	62
6	Hypnosis as an Adjunct to Chemotherapy in Cancer	77
7	A Guided Fantasy	88
8	Recent Experiences with Gestalt, Encounter and Hypnotic Techniques	97
9	The Evocative Power of Language	117
10	*The February Man* Foreword	122

11 *Hypnotherapy: An Exploratory Casebook* Foreword   128
12 *Stories for the Third Ear* Foreword   135

Index   *138*

FOREWORD

Sidney Rosen's important essays are a Rosetta stone, one which de-mystifies Milton Erickson's unconventional, and life changing, hypnotic learning and strategic therapy.

In May of 1977 after my own meeting, and studying, with Dr. Erickson in Phoenix, my life too unexpectedly changed positively, personally and professionally.

It was the mid-1980s that Dr. Rosen and I first met, when he invited me to speak at The New York Society for Ericksonian Psychotherapy and Hypnosis (NYSEPH), and we then became friends. After meeting many times thereafter in New York City, I came to know his gentle, brilliant, and humorous, ways of speaking and thinking. I am truly honored that he asked me to write this foreword to his book of brilliantly sensitive essays on hypnosis and psychotherapy.

In addition to being deeply changed by our different times learning with Milton Erickson—Rosen much longer, and more deeply, than I—Dr. Rosen and I unexpectedly discovered our similar love for Japanese culture. He went there after his military service in Korea, and I married into a Japanese family in the 1970s. We still speak our limited Japanese to each other when we connect by phone, or in person. It's our love for the heartful and delicate aesthetic, of Japanese culture that's deepened our friendship over time.

What I came to realize was that our mutual attraction to these delicate, aesthetic elements in Japanese art became a natural connecting thread to the poetic quality in therapeutic healing, qualities which we were both eager to learn from, and experiment with, in our professional work.

I came to hear the poetic voice in my daily life after coming from a gang dominated junior high school, and being fortunate enough to be accepted to a school for talented music and art students. I then learned it more deeply by sitting with and listening to poets Robert Frost and Allen Ginsberg.

Rosen shows us how, with Erickson, he came to recognize the importance of engaging a person's natural poetic sensibility in the therapeutic session. Let's look at this way of learning.

First, can we remember when we were taught to read poetry as literature in school? Now, compared to that, can we see the sound, and feeling, of *how we naturally speak what we're sensitively feeling in the moment, the living poetic?*

This living poetic is the heart of Erickson's teachings, and Rosen's essays.

The essence of Milton Erickson's work, as described in Rosen's essays, focuses on *how to engage, and enlist,* our client's natural attention by evoking their natural poetic learning state.

Once that's done, we can then guide them to apply it for resolving their personal problems, which they can evoke, and use, for their personal growth outside the therapy room.

We see in Rosen's essays how Erickson, driven by his own physical limitations, unexpectedly discovered *new ways to teach himself how to learn*; ways he brought into the trance work he pioneered and brought into his unconventional therapeutic practice.

For example, let's take a moment to imagine the sound of Dr. Rosen's voice outside the justified margins of the printed word on the page from one of his essays. Here's a paragraph from his essay, "What Makes Ericksonian Therapy So Effective."

This is how it appears in the justified margins on the page:

> When a person entered into Erickson's sphere, he entered into a new reality—a world of magic, of childhood, and of whimsical humor. In this atmosphere we are likely to revert to childlike responses, to childlike openness to learning, and to the malleability of childhood. When a therapist can create a world of wonder, of freshness of view, his patients are likely to respond with the "suggestibility" of children. Therapeutic suggestions and role modeling are bound to be more effective than they would be if presented only to the conscious, logical, "left brain" mind.

Now, from my having sat with, listened to, and spoken with Sid Rosen over many hours, let's look at the above as I "heard him" telling it to me almost in person, through the natural poetic of Rosen's spoken voice:

> When a person entered into Erickson's sphere,
> he entered into a new reality
> a world of magic,
> of childhood,
> and of whimsical humor.
> In this atmosphere
> we are likely to revert
> to childlike responses,

> to childlike openness to learning,
> and to the malleability of childhood.
> When a therapist can create a world of wonder,
> of freshness of view,
> his patients are likely to respond
> with the "suggestibility" of children.
> Therapeutic suggestions and role modeling
> are bound to be more effective
> than they would be, if presented
> only to the conscious, logical, "left brain" mind.

This is his feelingful way of poetically speaking, the one that Erickson, and Rosen, learned to access, and bring forth from their clients' lives.

In Rosen's essays he shows us how this natural poetic of our spoken voice changes our experience from our externally focused, rapid, thinking style, to our slower, more imaginary, feelingful way of reflecting on our lives.

Since, as Ralph Waldo Emerson wrote, "The poem is written in the moment of reflection," so did Erickson, and Rosen, capture, and engage, this uniquely important slow, poetic, reflective learning state in their client's lives. Rosen's essays show us how clients consciously learned to access their self-learning ability, to learn new ways to appreciate, and be, themselves, in their lives.

By listening to the natural poetic of our spoken voice we gain access to the way of learning that is the essence of the Ericksonian learning experience.

As we see in his foreword to *The February Man*, Rosen shows us that by helping clients slow themselves poetically down, the therapist becomes a facilitator for clients becoming their own best teachers. We can almost hear the sound of Rosen's voice in these words.

> "It is the patient who does the work. All that the therapist does is to provide conditions in which this work can be done." Erickson worked thoroughly and carefully to provide the necessary conditions.

And later, Rosen writes,

> Thus, he, (Erickson) demonstrated the respect which was the hallmark of his way of dealing with patients. In fact, we must comment at this point that, although much of the writing about "Ericksonian techniques" emphasizes the brilliance and ingenuity of the therapist, when we observe Erickson, himself, at work, we are impressed more by the presence and the unique creativity of his patients.

And, finally, in his essay foreword to *Hypnotherapy: An Exploratory Casebook* Rosen writes:

Many therapists, both psychoanalytic and others, will find his (Erickson's) approaches compatible with their own and far removed from their preconceptions about hypnosis. As the authors point out, hypnosis does not change the person nor does it alter past experiential life. It serves to permit him to learn more about himself and to express himself more adequately.... Therapeutic trance helps people side-step their own learned limitations so that they can more fully explore and utilize their potentials.

These are just a few examples of the gems of therapeutic learning, and skills, that you will find throughout Sidney Rosen's essays in this book.

Thank you, Sidney Rosen, for giving us a Rosetta Stone demystifying Dr. Erickson's, and your own, poetic ways of hypnotic learning; ways that help us live more heartfully richer lives, both within ourselves, and with those we love. Thank you.

Melvyn Bucholtz, MA
Santa Fe, NM
August 2018

INTRODUCTION

The idea for this book began when Dr. Rosen and I were sitting for lunch at Timmy's by the River. Our friendship began in the early 1990s and over the years he has been a wonderful guide and mentor for me. As we sat there together that day, I mentioned I had been rereading several of his writings, all of which I find to be remarkable jewels of wisdom, clarity and hope. I thought what a great idea it would be to have them all in one place. That one volume would be a Rosetta Stone for any and all interested in the art of psychotherapy and the artistry of Milton H. Erickson. Dr. Rosen agreed and off we went. Now as I think back on it, I wonder if it was really my idea or a hypnotic suggestion by Dr. Rosen!

Dr. Rosen is co-author with Milton Erickson of *My Voice Will Go with You: The Teaching Tales of Milton Erickson* and the Founding President of the New York Milton H. Erickson Society for Hypnosis and Psychotherapy (NYSEPH). He conducted workshops on Ericksonian approaches in the United States and Europe. He was an Assistant Clinical Professor of Psychiatry at the New York University Medical Center and NYU Hospital and on the American Institute for Psychoanalysis faculty. Also, for over 40 years he had a significant private practice in New York City.

The following chapters by Dr. Rosen are essential reading for those who seek to learn essential elements of psychotherapy. They elucidate fundamental aspects of Erickson's approaches and outline factors effective in all forms of psychotherapy. They contain core teachings of many central and timeless elements in psychotherapy.

The first chapter, *Values and Philosophy of Milton H. Erickson,* walks through the root values a therapist can use to underpin his approach, his interventions, and the goals to which he leads his client—uniqueness, optimism, the unconscious, the role of imagination, learning and doing, and much, much more. Dr. Rosen provides personal insights that reflect Milton Erickson's wit, wisdom, and humor.

For example, Rosen advises us to lead life with an "innocent eye," so that every moment contains a potential surprise.

The next chapter is *What makes Ericksonian Therapy so Effective*. Here, Dr. Rosen advises us that "we need to ask both what are we changing our client's to, as well as what we are moving them from." As Erickson put it, a therapist needs to be flexible, proactive and encouraging of small change, "substituting a good idea for a bad idea" and supporting the client to "start the snowball rolling."

We must know our tools as a surgeon would need to be completely familiar with the use of scalpel or forceps. For the therapist, the tools are words and non-verbal forms of communication. We must know how to capture attention and to do it so entirely that the client becomes "en-tranced" in what we are saying.

In *One Thousand Induction Techniques and Their Application to Therapy and Thinking*, we are led to realize that the critical element to hypnotic induction is the knowledge that *anytime a person focuses on one thing he or she will go into a trance*. With that we are exposed to the Early Learning Set Induction, an induction which combines trance, age-regression, and the seeding of therapeutic ideas.

Dr. Rosen advises that trance is a common element in effective therapy, be it psychoanalytic, cognitive, behavioral, solution-orientated, or relaxation. By illuminating the use of suggestion and trance in each of these, he underscores the importance of having understandings in communication and most especially evocative hypnotic communication. As all therapists and physicians are knowingly or unknowingly making suggestions to their clients or patients, with practiced awareness they can be able to make positive helpful suggestions. To illustrate, Rosen suggests to a patient undergoing chemotherapy, "You ought to get an increasing feeling of well-being and security as you realize that you have received an adequate dose of medication, perhaps after your third or fourth treatment, from the cumulative effect of the medication" in the chapter *Hypnosis as an Adjunct to Chemotherapy in Cancer*.

In the chapter *Concretizing of Symptoms and Their Manipulation,* Rosen instructs us that, at the unconscious level, thought occurs in images, metaphors, and symbols. He shows how a woman with a broken heart closes her eyes and sees the word LOVE broken into two, one part LO and another part VE. He suggests she repair the word by joining these parts together again, a process which heals her pain. Further examples are provided in dealing with abdominal pain, hair-pulling (Trichotillomania), and nausea from chemotherapy. In the process, he guides us on how to use the power of imagination to promote healing.

In the chapter *Psychotherapeutic and Hypnotherapeutic Approaches of Milton H. Erickson,* Rosen relates the story "Dry Beds" from his previous book, *My Voice Will Go with You: The Teaching Tales of Milton H. Erickson.* He uses the story to illuminate his basic approach that, "First you model the patient's world, then you role-model the patient's world." He advises us to learn the "patient's theoretical model" and "utilizing the patient's own language, not the language of any doctrine or school."

The chapter *A Guided Fantasy* is a verbatim group induction. The induction includes truisms, dissociations, relaxation, age regression and metaphors interspersed with suggestions to "get in touch with unconscious learnings, use those unconscious learnings, to find something there of value, of interest wherever we are, and climb as high as [we] want." When the group is awakened from Rosen's induction, they return rested, enlightened, self-caring and optimistic for the days ahead, a remarkable journey indeed!

In the chapter *Recent Experiences with Gestalt, Encounter and Hypnotic Techniques*, Rosen reviews the different approaches and builds towards his conclusion that the therapist must be active, must conduct therapy or else no therapy will take place. His cases demonstrate Rosen's ability to create evocative transforming patient experiences from which patients are brought to action, because "patients move best when they are moved."

The chapter entitled *Evocative Power of Language* is Rosen's contribution to the *Collected Works of Kay Thompson*. Kay was a talented hypnotherapist and dentist who also studied with Erickson and was widely recognized as a master hypnotist as well as a woman of great wisdom. Here Rosen teaches us that we learn from and by experience and that experiences can arise both from the real world and the world of our imagination. So, therapists must aim to make their language so entrancing that the patient experiences it at a sufficiently deep level, that it evokes in them a reality they are actually experiencing in the now.

The last three chapters are forewords to *The February Man*, *Hypnotherapy*, and *Stories for the Third Ear*. Each one is a remarkably beautiful gem of wisdom, guidance, and optimism. Here one finds a succinct refreshment of the clear and simple ideas that can propel you towards renewed energy, excitement and dedication: "In my way of living I often like to climb a mountain—and I always wonder what's on the other side," or the Sufi saying, "Speak to the wall so the door may hear." We hear how Erickson in his own work strove to make an interesting design of therapy, never seeking to solve a problem in an old way, if he could think of a new way. We are reminded of this by Rosen's first book, *My Voice Will Go with You: The Teaching Tales of Milton H. Erickson* and Erickson's use of metaphors and stories to convey ideas in a fashion that is gentle, entrancing, and enjoyable.

I hope I have shared in some way my excitement for this book and my enthusiasm for the enjoyment, wisdom, guidance, and specific techniques you will find here. These are truly remarkable writings on psychotherapy, applied by one of Erickson's finest students, who was also a dedicated and experienced therapist.

Victor Kiarsis, LMSW, MBA
Rye, New York
August 2018

ACKNOWLEDGEMENTS

The joy of a project such as this is the wonderful people that join in along the path to help, contribute, and support the effort in kind and sometimes unexpected ways. And there are many people to whom we owe a debt of thanks for their contributions, for without their assistance this work would not be where it is today.

We are fortunate that Melvyn Bucholtz agreed to provide a wonderful foreword. Melvyn is a longtime friend of Dr. Rosen and has been an outstanding supporter of the project. His support in seeing the beauty, artistry and essential knowledge of Dr. Rosen's writings has been a continual source of encouragement. Melvyn's relationships with Dr. Rosen and also with Milton H. Erickson, his in-depth knowledge of psychotherapy and hypnotherapy along with his healing and caring presence, have enriched the project.

We were also blessed to have Dr. Rosen's son, Jeffrey Rosen, contribute to the project. Jeffrey is the President and CEO of the National Constitution Center in Philadelphia, an author of seven books and a commentator on legal and constitutional issues in various media, including radio, TV and podcasts. Somehow in all of that he found time to assist his father in preparing chapter introductions. It has been a distinct pleasure to get to know Jeffrey and to benefit from his deep professional knowledge, his skills and his deeply caring personality.

A critical moment in the project's life was when we connected with Nina Guttapalle, Editor at Routledge/Taylor & Francis. Nina was truly the wind beneath our wings and it was her confidence and commitment to the project that were the essential elements in where we are today.

Finally, I was blessed to have a wonderful wife, Karen, and supportive family, who at every turn, encouraged, helped, and urged me on. Without them none of this would have been possible.

PHOTOS

Sidney Rosen, M.D. – a healer at work

Milton H. Erickson M.D. with Sidney Rosen M.D.

M. H. Erickson at work in his Phoenix home

A holiday greeting from the Erickson family

Sidney Rosen at the Erickson home with Milton Erickson and Ernest Rossi (circa 1970)

ORIGINAL ARTICLE PUBLICATIONS

"The Values and Philosophy of Milton H. Erickson," in Ericksonian Approaches to Hypnosis and Psychotherapy, edited by Jeffrey Zeig. 1982. Chapter 41, pages 462–476.

"What Makes Ericksonian Therapy So Effective?" in Developing Ericksonian Therapy: State of the Art, edited by Jeffrey Zeig and Stephen R. Lankton. 1988. Chapter 1, pages 5–21.

"One thousand Induction Techniques and Their Application to Therapy and Thinking" in Ericksonian Methods: The Essence of the Story, edited by Jeffrey Zeig. 1994. Chapter 22, pages 333–348.

"Concretizing of Symptoms and Their Manipulation" in Brief Therapy Myths, Methods and Metaphors, edited by Jeffrey Zeig and Stephen Gilligan. 1990. Chapter 20, pages 258–272.

"The Psychotherapeutic and Hypnotherapeutic Approaches of Milton H. Erickson," American Journal of Psychoanalysis, Vol. 44, No. 2, 1984.

"Hypnosis as an Adjunct to chemotherapy in Cancer," in Ericksonian Psychotherapy II: Clinical Applications, edited by Jeffrey Zeig, 1985. Chapter 28, pages 387–398.

"A Guided Fantasy", in Ericksonian Hypnotherapeutic Group Inductions, edited by Hildegard and Klippstein. 1991. Chapter 18, pages 129–135.

"Recent experiences with gestalt, encounter and hypnotic techniques," American Journal of Psychoanalysis, Vol. 32, No. 1, March 1972.

"The Evocative Power of Language," in The Art of Therapeutic Communication, The Collected Works of Kay F. Thompson, edited by Saralee Kane, MSW and Karen Olness M.D. 2004.

"Foreword," in The February Man: Evolving Consciousness and Identity in Hypnotherapy, by Milton H. Erickson and Ernest Rossi. 1989.

"Foreword," in Hypnotherapy: An Introductory Casebook, by Milton H. Erickson and Ernest Rossi. 1979.

"Foreword," in Stories for the Third Ear, by Lee Wallas. 1985.

1

THE VALUES AND PHILOSOPHY OF MILTON H. ERICKSON[1]

Introduction

Milton Erickson's values came from his observations of the uniqueness of each individual. Erickson's experience taught him to resist generalizations, stereotypes, and labels, and to refuse to put individuals into categories or boxes. For him the differences among people were as important as the similarities, a value vividly captured by the allergist who noticed the differences among every blade of grass. This emphasis on the uniqueness of each individual contributed to his realistic, moderate, and ultimately optimistic view of life: because he encouraged the value of difference, he looked at each moment with an innocent eye, as a source of potential delight and surprise. Although patients could feel Erickson's optimism and his sense of wonder and joy in the possibilities of fulfilling individual potential, Erickson did not embrace unrealistic abstractions or romantic idealizations. Instead, his optimism was rooted in the importance of recognizing and accepting human limitations.

"It is only when working within limitations that the master is disclosed," Goethe wrote. Erickson, too, believed that only by accepting limitations could individuals learn and grow and realize their untapped potential. Perhaps the central value that emerges from Erickson's thought is that, by realistically accepting our limitations, all of us can discover that "you know much more than you think you know." Recognizing that we can't have everything, we can also discover that our boundaries are broader than we know as well. This balance shows Erickson's realism, and allows individuals to deal with the world realistically.

Erickson's emphasis on reality, on living in the here and now, led him to focus not on achieving our untapped potential, or what we might achieve, but instead on recognizing and enjoying what we have now. Imagine you are walking along a path and reach a cleft from an earthquake in the ground. If you refuse to accept the reality that the cleft is in front of you, you could walk into it. If you accept the reality of the cleft, you can devise ways of avoiding it or going around it. Erickson always wanted to know what individuals could do in a particular situation, not what they would like to do in their dreams.

Erickson rejected parapsychology as not being based in reality and was not himself a practitioner of organized religion. But individuals experienced him as spiritual because of his acceptance of the mystical aspects of life that cannot be explained by the conscious mind. Describing dreams, he said, "the unexplainable fits into the realm of the spirit."

For Erickson, an emphasis on mindfulness in the here and now can help individuals be fully present and enjoy their lives. Focusing on the details of flowers, mushrooms, and birds can give us pleasurable experiences, and Erickson himself emphasized pleasurable sensations, as opposed to the physical pain he himself experienced for much of his life. One of the last times I saw Erickson, I asked him, "How are you, Milton?" He said, "If I could cry, Sid, I would." My response: "It's painful, but if you consider the alternatives, you prefer to experience the pain, don't you?" He nodded.

Erickson loved to have fun with his family—he was always a prankster as well as a teacher—and until the end, he never lost his optimism, his acceptance of reality, and his sense of humor. All this was embodied in his response to a story soon before his death that he was about to die. "I think that is entirely premature," Erickson responded. "I have no intention of dying. In fact, that's the last thing I'm going to do."

***

When we observe and examine the work of Milton Erickson, we must conclude that he was one of the most effective manipulators in the field of psychotherapy. Was he therefore a dangerous man—and are his admirers and followers likely to propagate harmful, self-aggrandizing movements? Most of us realize that it is not possible to be with others, psychotherapeutically or otherwise, without influencing them. The "value-free" approaches of psychoanalysis are obviously far from that goal. Therefore, we understand that therapists who do not consciously "manipulate" their patients are still influencing them and that the type of influence must be determined by the "kind of person" the therapist is—his manner, physical appearance, dress, and way of living. Under all of these attributes must lie his value system. Many therapists are not at all explicit about their value systems or even aware of them. In judging whether Erickson was dangerous or helpful, meddlesome or wise, we are not confronted with this vagueness. In over 150 papers, he was most explicit and accurate in reporting what he actually said and did with patients. We can review some of these papers and tape recordings of actual sessions and derive a rather consistent picture of his values and life goals. He was often explicit about his own values in his teaching sessions. I have had the privilege of discussing his values with him, with Betty Erickson, and with the Erickson children. Still, of course, any interpretations in this chapter are my own.

Uniqueness of the Individual

Most philosophers, psychologists, anthropologists, and other scientists who examine the human condition, and even those who examine nature, have emphasized similarities and have grouped phenomena according to their similarities. For example, almost every psychologist or psychoanalyst has a theory of personality or character types. This tendency goes back to ancient days when the various temperaments were divided according to the elements as they were then seen: earth, fire, water, and air. In modern times, Freud grouped personality types (as later elaborated by Abraham) according to stages of psychosexual development into oral, anal, phallic, and genital types. Erich Fromm divided people into the marketing personality, the hoarding type, and others. His concept of the productive personality was equivalent to Freud's genital type. Karen Horney defined a morbid dependent type of personality, an arrogant-vindictive, and a detached type. Even in ordinary conversation we tend to type people-as geniuses, lazy bums, alcoholics, work addicts. Then, when we look at a particular person, we tend to see him in a narrow way.

Erickson's approach was different. He emphasized the differences between people, the uniqueness of each individual and even of each object. This emphasis is exemplified by his story of the allergist whom he told to sit in a field. After about three hours, the allergist returned to Erickson and said, "Did you know that every blade of grass is a different shade of green?" In telling this story, Erickson was pointing up the value of noting distinctions. Every person has different shades of any characteristic that we can define. Erickson encouraged us to treasure those unique shades.

In many stories, Erickson emphasized the value of his own differences from others, especially as manifested in his physical defects—color blindness, dyslexia, lack of sense of rhythm, and so on. Although most of us do not have so many obvious outer manifestations of difference from others, certainly we are all aware of thoughts and points of view that we assume are markedly different from the "normal." Erickson encouraged us to value these differences.

Optimism

He encouraged people to look at themselves and to treasure not only their differences from others, but also differences between their present and past behavioral patterns. This very emphasis on these latter differences, in contrast to others' emphasis on our tendency towards repetition, may be the prime factor leading to Erickson's optimistic view of life. For him, every day, every moment, offered an opportunity for new beginnings. This optimism is illustrated in his statement that in playing golf or any other game one ought to approach each shot as if it was the first one. Thereby one forgets previous attempts, previous tensions, previous failures, and even previous successes.

"Since we do not know what the next moment will bring, what tomorrow will bring," Erickson pointed out, "life is not something you can give an answer to today. You should enjoy the process of waiting, the process of becoming what you are. There is nothing more delightful than planting flower seeds and not knowing what kind of flowers are going to come up."

With regard to goals he said, "You encourage patients to do all those simple little things that are their own right as growing creatures. You see, we don't know what our goals are. We learn our goals only in the process of getting there." As his young daughter said once, when he asked what she was making, "I don't know what I'm building, but I'm going to enjoy building it. When I'm through building it, I'll know what it is!" As he said, "You don't know what a baby is going to become. Therefore, you wait and take good care of it until it becomes what it will."

This approach leads to looking at life with what I call the "innocent eye," with every moment being a potential surprise. Terms such as "surprise" and "delight" commonly were used by Erickson. With this way of looking at life's phenomena, one is more likely to feel optimistic than pessimistic. Certainly, pessimism is promoted by the conviction that we are bound to repeat the same destructive and boring patterns to which we have been conditioned, and Erickson was aware of both the value and the limitations imposed upon us by our conditioned patterns. Yet, more than most therapists he emphasized the positive.

The Wisdom of the Unconscious

As Jay Haley pointed out in *Uncommon Therapy*,

> Unlike psychodynamically oriented therapists who make interpretations to bring out negative feelings and hostile behavior, Erickson relabels what people do in a positive way, to encourage change. He does not minimize the difficulties, but he will find in the difficulties some aspect of them that can be used to improve the functioning of a person or his family.
>
> (Haley, 1973, p. 34)

Haley related this emphasis on the positive to the fact that Erickson worked in a framework of hypnosis and that while others felt a distrust of those ideas outside of conscious and rational awareness, hypnotists made up another large stream of therapists who emphasized that the unconscious was a positive force.

In fact, if Erickson and his followers have any "religious" guide or belief, it must be in the wisdom of the unconscious. He believed that people can be guided by and can trust their own unconscious minds to determine what is best in any particular moment and in general. Even during hypnotic inductions he expressed this trust and belief by saying such things as, "Go as deeply into a trance as you wish." He believed that people have the capacity and the resources to comfort and heal themselves. As he once advised a therapist who was treating an adult patient, "You can regress her to 11 years of age and then have her, as a separate person, comfort that 11-year old girl as herself comforting herself." He felt there was always something constructive, even in the most foreboding or apparently sterile or destructive situation. He expressed this belief in an indirect hypnotic induction which began, "In my way of living, I often like to climb a mountain. I always wonder what's on the other side. On my side of the mountain may be meadows, hills, rivers and on the other side, there may be a desert, dark and foreboding." He concluded, "And I would know that however harsh and foreboding a desert was, I would find something there of interest to me."

Imagination

Like Blake and Yeats, Erickson placed a high value on "imagination" or our capacity to form inner images. In modern times, the word "imagination" has become denigrated. We must go back to Blake and Yeats in order to understand the connection of this word with words such as "vision," "visionary," "imagery." Bronowski writes, "In my view, which not everyone shares, the central problem of human consciousness depends on the ability to imagine" (Bronowski, 1978, p. 18). In his work with hypnosis, Erickson had discovered that by evoking imagery it was often possible to help patients change. Mere intellectual recollection often was ineffective. This emphasis on imagery, which after all is itself a form of experiencing, is connected with another value that Erickson emphasized, viz., *experience is essential*.

He would not want anybody to accept his philosophy or any of his statements because he had said them or because they were published in some book. In fact, he taught that "Therapy cannot be learned from books. It is learned from life." Erickson told me, "I received a letter from a woman last week which told about her daughter becoming six years old. The next day she did something her mother reprimanded her for and she made the remark, 'It's awfully hard to be six years old. I've only had one day's experience.'"

Protection of the Patient

Although he believed in the tendency of the unconscious mind to protect the conscious, Erickson felt that it is incumbent upon the therapist, who temporarily may be given the power to override this protective function, to himself protect the patient. He noted,

> The patient does not come to you just because you are a therapist. The patient comes to be protected or helped in some regard. But the personality

is very vital to the person, and he doesn't want you to do too much, he does not want you to do it too suddenly. You've got to do it gradually and you've got to do it in the order in which he can assimilate.

He would time his interventions according to the responses of his patient. When he said, "You've got to do it gradually," he obviously meant that you must allow the patient time and scope to move and grow, based on his own unconscious wisdom. He also felt that people's privacy must be protected against the intrusion of others. When he gave a demonstration before a group, he would always ask his subject to reveal, "Only that which you can share with strangers." When I called him and asked him to coauthor our book, *My Voice Will Go with You: Teaching Tales of Milton H. Erickson* (Rosen, 1982), his first response was, "We must protect the individuals who are described."

Betty commented on her husband's desire for privacy:

> Milton always took a dim view, and I have exactly the same feeling too, of having his biography written. He had a strong feeling of privacy that there are things in your life, experiences, beliefs and relationships that were just nobody's business.

Betty recalled that he had said that if he wrote his autobiography, he would either have to disguise or alter the things that he didn't think he would ever want written down or else he would have to make it so "wishy washy" that it would be uninteresting.

Assets and Limitations

We all know that Erickson believed strongly in utilizing whatever one had, including characteristics normally labeled as "handicaps." He also pointed out the importance of recognizing and accepting one's limitations. When I went to see him in 1970, asking him to use hypnosis to help me improve my memory for names, he made several comments to the effect that, "You know much more than you think you know." He then shared with me the information that he also had a poor memory for names and in fact for other information as well. He illustrated this with

> Here, in this office, I remember everything that is relevant about a patient. But, if I meet the patient outside of the office, I may not recall anything about him—even his name. The memory for this information belongs here—here in this office.

Later in that same session with me, he interjected an apparently irrelevant comment, "And at my mother's funeral, my father remarked, 'It was nice to have 73 wedding anniversaries with one person. It would have been nicer to have 74— but you can't have everything.'"

Erickson's Ideas on the Supernatural and ESP

Generally speaking, Erickson, like Houdini, dismissed so called supernatural and ESP-type experiences as being based on trickery, illusion, or highly developed observational powers. His attitude was summarized in a letter to Dr. Ernest F. Pecci, dated June 8, 1979, in which he wrote:

> I feel that I should inform you that I do not believe that the field of parapsychology is scientifically established and I also feel that the so-called evidence for the existence of these faculties is based on false mathematical logic, misinterpretation of data, overlooking of minimal sensory cues, bias in interpretation and frequently on outright fraud. I have worked for over fifty years to disassociate the study of hypnosis from mystical and unscientific connotations.

He added, "Extensive experience and examination of evidence from a scientific perspective, likewise, makes me believe that so-called hypnotic regression to early infancy and to the womb are pure fantasy."

He liked to tell about the times when he had fooled fortune tellers. He accomplished this by feeding them false information through the medium of subvocal speech! Apparently, some fortune tellers, like Erickson himself, are able to read subvocal speech. He also told me about how he had deceived J.B. Rhine by looking at Rhine's cards from such an angle that he could see the light reflections on the back of the cards. He explained that the original cards were stamp impressed, and the diamond or star patterns could be seen if they were viewed from the right angle. He told me also about a patient who was able to identify cards by memorizing the very slight irregularities on the back of a regular deck of cards.

Erickson had developed his senses to the point that he could listen to a typewriter and often pick out the individual letters from their sound. He even learned to recognize the typing patterns of his various secretaries to the point that he could frequently tell whether the secretary was premenstrual, menstrual, or postmenstrual. He also could sometimes tell when a secretary had had intercourse the night before. When I asked him where he got the data for this last interpretation, he explained that he would check with the secretary's husband. If both he and his wife were in a good mood that day, he would correlate this information and he would also correlate it with the typing patterns. "It's just that people are so expressive," Erickson commented, "Yet we are never trained to read these expressions."

When I asked Erickson for his opinion on so-called supernatural phenomena he said,

> Well, there is a simple thing about religion, the soul, and mysticism. The cave man slept like you and I, and yet his daily life experience was very different. He fought with the bear, and in his dreams he fought hard and

long with the bear. And in the morning there was no bear to be seen. It was a spirit bear! The unexplainable fits into the realm of "spirit."

Betty told me,

> Milton had the deepest respect for intellectual solutions and the sort of mind that can put together a problem, intellectually, and just cut through to the heart of it. But he was outraged by people who would call themselves scientists and yet would immediately accept the supernatural or paranormal explanations for something, without examining the possibility that the phenomena could be explained according to accepted laws of nature. He liked to refer people to "Occam's Razor"; William of Occam stated that you don't postulate an explanation unnecessarily, when a phenomenon can be explained in terms of known relationships.

Betty added, "Milton felt that many people were far too gullible about things like healing by the laying on of hands." The sensations that some practitioners have reported, which have convinced them that some real energy is transmitted in this procedure, can easily be produced by autosuggestion.

Out-of-body experiences, Betty felt, can be explained by the loss of the background sensations that are present during normal consciousness and which used to be called "coenesthesia." These sensations often fade away when a person enters into a trance or when a person is in a precomatose state. The lack of coenesthesia at these times is interpreted as the spirit departing from the body.

Religion

Before going to college Erickson was raised in an old-fashioned farm community, in the Methodist Church. When he broadened his knowledge of the world he moved away from conventional organized religion. As Betty told me, "His feeling was that you should lead as decent and productive a life as you could, and he didn't bother worrying about transcendental questions. These were matters that couldn't be answered definitely, so he didn't try to answer them." A patient of mine had been told by a Sufi teacher, who incidentally had previously been a psychiatrist that, next to the leader of his sect, the most spiritual person in the world was Milton Erickson. When I told Betty, she replied, "Milton would have been highly amused by that." Additionally, Betty pointed out that even though he was not religious in the conventional sense, "He never tried to dissuade anyone. His patients and students certainly felt free to express their own beliefs."

Learning and Doing

Even when he was discussing subjects such as death, Erickson would always instill the injunction, "Enjoy your life." He knew of course that not all things in life were enjoyable and would cite his mother's favorite quotation from Longfellow, "Into each life some rain must fall. Some days must be dark and dreary," but his main focus was on the enjoyment of life. He believed that two activities promoted this enjoyment more than anything else—learning and doing.

Learning about oneself and about the world, he felt, was good, pleasant, and satisfying. Learning new things about oneself is pleasing, so long as one is guided by principles of interest and curiosity. It need not be frightening or anxiety-provoking. In *Uncommon Therapy*, he stated, "I don't believe in salvation only through pain and suffering" (Haley, 1973, p. 282).

Along these same lines, curiosity and wanting to know are good. He once told a patient, "You had a dream with a lot of affect. Now I don't know if you want to find out the cognitive side of that today, tomorrow, or next week, or perhaps later this year." He then explained that he had given her a choice, and he added, "I have human curiosity working for me."

The other great source of pleasure is *doing*. Erickson was not anti-intellectual. But he was certainly anti-intellectualizing. Especially with overly obsessive detached patients, he found it important to encourage them to get away from books and to do things. He would often say, "Get all of your hard work done as soon as possible so the last 40 years of your life will be happy." He might add, "You can have plenty of bad luck come your way, for free. If you want something in life, you have to earn it."

Erickson emphasized that it was not only important to do things but what one does must have social consequences. In his beautiful story of the depressed woman whom he encouraged to cultivate African violets (Zeig, 1980), he pointed out that his patient not only recovered from her depression, but that she always had African violets to *give*, as gifts for weddings, funerals, christenings, and other occasions. He concluded, "When she died, in her 70s, of natural causes, she was known as the 'African violet queen of Milwaukee.' And she had an endless number of friends."

Erickson encouraged and arranged for productivity even in mental hospitals. Jay Haley tells of a patient in a mental hospital who believed that he was Jesus Christ. Erickson said to him, "I understand you have some skill in carpentry" (Haley, 1973). When the patient admitted that he had, Erickson put him to work building bookcases. Subsequently, the patient was able to do other productive work and eventually to leave the hospital, free of delusions and self-supporting. Erickson was opposed to people's accepting welfare aid except temporarily and when it was absolutely necessary. Even then, his sense of fairness led him to believe that they should pay back in money or in some other way for any help that was received. He illustrated this with the story of a maid he had hired when he first came to Arizona. He said,

> She was a widow with six small children. She had been in the hospital, having her sixth child, and her husband was killed. She went on welfare for a

year. During that time she learned to read and write, and she then got a job as a maid. She paid back all the welfare money and supported her children.

I witnessed a session in which he told a patient that he would not charge her anything because she could not afford it. He also told her that she could not afford to stay in Phoenix and that she should return home immediately. She should insist that her child's father pay a reasonable child support, and she should work, even at such things as embroidery and typing, in order to support herself. He was very emphatic in his insistence that the only way she would get over her unhappiness would be to do things that were productive rather than wasting her time in self-examination and soul-searching.

Manipulation

Erickson pointed out that he had often been accused of manipulating patients—to which he replied,

> Every mother manipulates her baby if she wants it to live. Every time you go to a store, you manipulate the clerk to do your bidding, and when you go to a restaurant, you manipulate the waiter. And the teacher in school manipulated you into learning to read and write. In fact, life is one big manipulation. The final manipulation is putting you to rest, and that is manipulation too. They have to lower the coffin, and then they have to get the ropes out—all manipulation. And you manipulate a pencil to write, to record thoughts. And you manipulate yourself, carrying around peanuts or cigarettes or Life Savers.

In other words, Erickson would equate what some people call manipulation with what others call exploration, experimentation, and mastery—of words, objects and situations. As I have mentioned above, in manipulating others he was always careful to avoid exploiting them, harming them in any way, or allowing them to harm themselves.

Raising Children

How did Erickson raise his children so that they could "manipulate" effectively? I believe that he accomplished this mainly by setting an example, especially in the handling of them. Betty Erickson agreed with my impression that Milton was a rather strict disciplinarian. She explained,

> I think that is correct—that he was rather strict and believed when you laid down the rules, you enforced them. I think I suffered sometimes more than the kids did. But, I learned to just leave the room and keep my opinion to myself because, you know, his approach always seemed to work, even though it wasn't the way I would do it.

I'll give you one of my favorite stories, about his disciplining of two-and-a-half-year-old Kristi, as he told it.

> One Sunday, we were reading the newspaper—all of us—and she walked up to her mother, grabbed the newspaper, threw it on the floor. Her mother said, "Kristi, that wasn't very nice. Pick up the paper and give it back to Mother. Tell her you are sorry."
>
> "I don't has to," Kristi said.
>
> Every member of the family gave her the same advice and got the same reply. So I told Betty to pick her up and put her in the bedroom. "I lay down on the bed, and she put Kristi beside me. Kristi looked at me contemptuously and started to scramble off. But I had a hold on her ankle. She said, "Wet Woose!"
>
> I said, "I don't has to."
>
> And that lasted four hours. She kicked and struggled. Pretty soon she freed one ankle. I got hold of the other. It was a desperate fight, like a silent fight between two Titans. At the end of four hours, she knew that she was the loser, and she said, "I will pick up the paper and give it to Mother."
>
> And that's where the ax fell. I said, "You don't has to."
>
> So she threw her brain into higher gear and said, "I will pick up the paper. I will give it to Mother. I will tell Mother I am sorry."
>
> And I said, "You don't has to."
>
> And then she shifted into full gear, "I will pick up the paper. I want to pick up the paper. I want to tell Mother I am sorry."
>
> I said, "Fine."

That is a beautiful illustration of the development of superego, isn't it?

Erickson showed the same kind of insistence in teaching his son to keep his word about taking out the garbage, repeatedly waking Robert up in the middle of the night, apologizing that he had forgotten to remind him to do this task during the day. Erickson emphasized that this kind of teaching of responsibility and limits is more easily done when the child is young. He would, however, treat grown patients in ways to ensure that they learned first to accept and then to incorporate authority. For example, we once asked him why he had insisted on sending a patient to climb Squaw Peak before he would do any other therapy with her. We wondered whether it was in order for her to get a feeling of accomplishment. Was it for her to get in touch with her own inner feelings of isolation?

And his answer was simply, "So that she would obey me." He had to establish obedience before he could direct her to do other things that would enable her to overcome the limitations of her phobic reaction.

Now, of course, we all know that authority can be misused, can be used cruelly, exploitatively, insensitively, and destructively. We also know from the ways in which Erickson's patients have developed inner-directedness and productive ways of living that he did not misuse his authority with them. Certainly, his children have not turned out to be either overly compliant or overly rebellious. Any contact with them indicates that they are well-balanced, happy, productive, and healthy. They have learned to take responsibility for their own lives, and they have passed on these same ethics to their own children.

Marriage

In spite of some people's idea to the contrary, Erickson did not rigidly hold to the belief that marriage was sacred and had to be sustained, regardless of the unhappiness of the participants. Zeig recorded a story about a couple, both psychiatrists, who returned home from a visit to Erickson and immediately dissolved their marriage of more than 15 years (Zeig 1980). In addition, each one fired his or her psychoanalyst. Interestingly, the psychoanalyst (they were both being treated by the same analyst) *himself* came with his wife to see Erickson, and the two of *them* were divorced immediately after this visit. Erickson pointed out that they maintained very friendly, mutually respecting relationships after their divorce. He mostly was concerned that each person lead a happy life and that he make intelligent choices, taking responsibility for these choices.

Attitudes to Women

As Betty told me, "Erickson certainly felt that women should have every sort of opportunity and should be treated with complete fairness in the job market and elsewhere. He also felt very strongly that there is a basic biological and psychological difference between the sexes." He believed for example that there was a basic maternal biological urge. He would note that little girls in any culture who were not given conventional dolls would make them, even out of a stick of wood or from seaweed. He felt that this maternal behavior was so universal that, if it was learned, it was learned in the very earliest stage of life. He understood that later nurturing of children and caring for a home involved only a division of labor. This type of responsibility could be negotiated between husband and wife.

Racial and Genetic Differences

Erickson objected to the idea that racial or national characteristics were completely learned and cultural. He felt that in certain cultures anything that had definite survival value could have a basic biological substrate. For example, he noted that the Vietnamese child adopted by his daughter and son-in-law reacted to stress by withdrawing; she became rigid and silent and even shut her eyes. Erickson understood that for anyone, especially a woman, who lived in an area where for 400 years the group had to survive recurrent conflicts, there was survival value in fading into the background. There was the element of "survival of the quietest," and certain temperaments were likely to survive. Actually, Erickson felt that denial of genetic differences was not an effective way of counteracting prejudice; in fact, he loved the differences. He felt they should be heightened, not swept over, nor ironed out. Sometimes, of course, he felt that it was necessary for people to adjust to them.

Milton and Betty were very aware of the differences in their own children. For example, Allan from the time he could walk was a mathematician. When he was four years old, and the Ericksons were living at Eloise Hospital in Michigan, he decided to count the rails on the large iron rail fences on the grounds of the hospital. Betty told me that when she would send another child out to remind him to come home for lunch, he would put a stick in the fence to mark the place, then come racing home, with his eyes glowing, chanting the numbers. He is now a mathematician, working for the government.

Marijuana

Erickson opposed the use of marijuana largely because he felt that evidence indicated that it was associated with loss of motivation. He also felt that we would not know for quite a while whether it is physically harmless. He recalled that when he was young, tobacco had been considered absolutely harmless. In fact, some studies had shown that people who smoked moderately were in better shape than people who didn't smoke at all. (This may have been due to the fact that people who were not in good health were not as likely to smoke.)

Aldous Huxley had worked with Erickson as part of his interest in altered states of consciousness. He had once remarked to Erickson that he felt at times that the insight gained with drugs could be compared to going down into a deep ditch and then climbing up onto a ladder. You felt that you were seeing very far, but, actually, you were still below ground level. Drugs elevate you from a very low level but not to a height that you could reach without drugs.

Esthetics

Many people who have tried to imitate Erickson's approaches achieve some success even though they may apply them in mechanistic, programmed ways. However, they usually miss a very important element—the element of poetry and of music. You see this feature in his stories, which contain a classical beauty and elegance in their form, rhythm, and tone. There is poetry and beauty in some of his posthypnotic suggestions. For example, he would say, "You will see a flash of color." I was reminded of this particular suggestion while reading Yeats' poem *The Lake Isle of Innisfree*.

> There midnight's all a glimmer, and noon a purple glow.
> And evening's full of the linnet's wings.

I discovered, to my delight, that in the summer the linnet male has a bright crimson-red breast and crown. What a flash of color that would be!

Humor

Whoever saw the twinkle in Milton Erickson's eyes, or the secret smile on his face as he talked, or who has heard him chuckle about the many practical jokes that were played within his family knows the large role that humor played in Erickson's life. His own and his listener's laughter frequently punctuated his stories. His family shared his enjoyment of jokes, and they would often devote a great deal of time to the promotion of one of these jokes. After Erickson's memorial service his son Lance told me about some of the tricks and games Erickson would indulge in with his children, and Lance emphasized the fact that the family always liked to have fun. Of course, Erickson carried his love of humor to his death bed.

Death

During the two-week period before his death I told my acquaintances some of Erickson's stories about death and dying. My favorite was the joke that Erickson made in response to hearing that a former student of his had been concerned at the rumor that he was dying: Erickson had said, "There is a story going around I am about to die. I think that is entirely premature. I have no intention of dying. That's the last thing I am going to do."

I cannot summarize Milton Erickson's values and philosophy more concisely than author Gwynn Cravens did at our memorial service in New York, when she said, "There are thousands, if not tens of thousands of people, whom Erickson helped to discover the sweetness of everyday life, the joy of hard work, the use of the muscles, the senses, the heart, and the head." Salvador Minuchin wrote to Erickson after visiting him about a week before Erickson's death,

> I was tremendously impressed with the way in which you are able to look at simple moments and describe their complexity and at your trust in the capacity of human beings to harness a repertory of experiences they do not know they have.

Note

1 This chapter was previously published in *Ericksonian Approaches to Hypnosis and Psychotherapy*, 1982, edited by Jeffrey Zeig as Chapter 41, pp. 462–476.

References

Bronowski, J. (1978). *The Origins of Knowledge and Imagination*. New Haven: Yale University Press.

Erickson, M.H., and Rossi, E. (1979). *Hypnotherapy: An Exploratory Casebook*. New York: Irvington.

Haley, J. (1973). *Uncommon Therapy: The Psychiatric Techniques of Milton H. Erickson, M.D.* New York: W.W. Norton & Co., Inc.

Rosen, S. (ed.) (1982). *Voice Will Go with You: The Teaching Tales of Milton H. Erickson, M. D.* New York: Norton.

Zeig, J.K. (ed.) (1980). *A Teaching Seminar with Milton H Erickson.* New York: Brunner/Mazel.

2

WHAT MAKES ERICKSONIAN THERAPY SO EFFECTIVE?[1]

Introduction

What makes Ericksonian therapy so effective? Erickson used techniques such as novelty, experimentation, and humor to unleash the unconscious learning within all of us. "Hypnosis is the evocation and utilization of unconscious learnings," Erickson wrote (Erickson, 1982). In order to do therapy, he maintained, "First you model the patient's world, and then you role model the patient's world" (ibid.). The goal of therapy, in Erickson's view, was to allow patients to achieve a sense of self-mastery and optimism, and to live in the present. I would add the goal of allowing patients to expand their own learning, growth, and social contributions.

Erickson was realistic about encouraging incremental rather than transformative growth by helping patients realistically evaluate their own limitations. He would discover what can and can't be changed by seeing how individuals respond to suggestions for change, without a predetermined goal in advance. The therapist tries to open up the patient's potential for growth by leaving it up to the patient to determine what changes they can realistically attempt. All of Erickson's interventions—including suggestions by therapists and patients—are based on the idea that changes must be determined by the patient himself, because if a patient is trying to achieve his own potential, he must discover and define his own limitations and possibilities.

A patient may not be trying to achieve his potential, of course. Instead, he or she may be trying to achieve relief from pain or anxiety or depression. And, as Karen Horney recognized, patients often go into therapy not to cure their neurosis but to perfect their neurosis—in other words, to accept their neurotic compulsions and either live with them or alter them slightly through small changes. Erickson would sometimes encourage that modest approach. If a patient was compulsive about something—about counting, for example—instead of encouraging the abandonment of the compulsion to count, Erickson would instead teach him to count in a different way, altering unconscious patterns in the process.

For patients whose symptom was an inability to live according to their potential—because of pain or anxiety—Erickson allowed them to find their potential on their own, by tapping into unconscious knowledge that they may not have been aware they had. The growth takes place not because it is consciously sought, but because when you're able to get relief from anxiety or pain, you are freer to live in the present, to stay with a situation, and to discover that you know much more than you think you know. For this reason, Erickson encouraged patients not always to overcome their anxiety but to feel their anxiety, spurring them to change by minimal interventions such as reframing. If you seek to eliminate anxiety entirely, Erickson recognized, you may eliminate a person's motivation to achieve change through therapy. Erickson would say that relieving anxiety is not sufficient and the therapist negotiates with the patient about what is desired and what is possible. His willingness to experiment, his playful optimism, his realistic sense of human limitations and possibilities, and his insistence on measured change through tapping into unconscious learning—all these qualities made his therapy effective.

***

On November 16, 1986, the *New York Times* (Lindsey, 1986) featured a front-page article about a Mrs. Knight, who maintained that a 35,000-year-old man, Ramtha, "used her body to speak words of wisdom." This rather ordinary-looking, 40-year-old American woman commands a following of thousands and her long mesmerizing monologues are attended by hundreds of people who pay $400 each. Many of them feel that this is the best money they have ever spent.

After attending one of her seminars, George Hain, a millionaire businessman from Cheyenne, Wyoming,

> returned to Cheyenne (the next day), disposed of his five Burger King restaurants and moved to a rural area in northern California, where he is building a house that is shaped like a pyramid, he says, to "manifest the energy" of the universe.

However, one of her more skeptical observers reported, "She's either psychotic or she's a good actress. She's obviously a fake, but she sure is a spellbinder."

In our terms, she is able to enter into a trance, to do "automatic speaking," to influence large groups of people, and to voice oracular pronouncements, coupled with prophesies of doom for those who do not follow her advice. Can we, with all our education, training, hard work and sincere caring for our patients, inspire, guide and heal them more successfully than does Mrs. Knight or the hundreds of other gurus or the thousands of other "healers" and "channelers" who are offering their skills today? Mrs. Knight, with good old American entrepreneurial directness, says, "I'm not a guru.... This is a business." We claim that we are practicing a healing or a teaching profession. As professionals, we are constantly questioning ourselves and undergoing self-examination. We strive to improve our skills and help our patients more effectively.

I am not prepared at this time to discuss the intriguing question of our effectiveness in comparison with guides, healers, and gurus. Just comparing our effectiveness with other psychotherapists is enough of a challenge.

When I talk about "Ericksonian Therapy," I run into difficulties. I recall the comments that people would make to Erickson about hypnosis: "I know what hypnosis is now—it is suggestion!" "I know what hypnosis is—it is concern with body image." "I know—it is transference." "It is relationship." "It is regression." "It is dissociation." "It is focusing of attention." And Erickson would answer, "Is that a ... a ... a ... all?"

Probably every one of the hundreds of therapists and students who visited Erickson had his or her own idea of what was the central feature, the secret of hypnotherapy. At congresses such as this one, scholarly researchers and clinicians are still trying to pinpoint the true "jewel in the lotus." And we can imagine Erickson, saying to each one of us who believes that he or she has identified that central feature, "Is that a ... a ... a ... all?"

As I tried to put my finger on factors that make Ericksonian therapy so effective (and I realize that outside of meetings such as this Third International Congress I would not necessarily get universal agreement that it is "so effective"), I found myself coming up with the same kind of unsatisfying partial answers, answers such as these:

Ericksonian therapy is especially effective because it uses trance states which heighten suggestibility, and suggestion is a major element in all psychotherapies. Or, Ericksonian therapy is especially effective because it allows for and encourages experimentation on the part of therapist and patient. Because of the concept of reframing. Because of its emphasis on health and resources rather than pathology. Because of its focus on goals, rather than genesis. Because it applies "systems thinking." Because ... because ...

I despaired that, even if we could agree that there is such an entity as "Ericksonian psychotherapy" and that it is so effective, we would be unlikely to be able to pin down one or two elements that lead to its being "so effective."

In this chapter I will discuss some of the more demonstrable or observable elements in the therapies which each of us devises for himself or herself, based on what we think we have learned directly and indirectly from the writings and teachings of Milton Erickson. And, after finishing this self-indulgence, I expect Milton to have his voice go with me, asking, with a chuckle, "Is that a ... a ... a ... all?"

Still, I will proceed with my observations and theses, which are based on my own experience of almost 40 years of exploring the effects of many different approaches to psychotherapy. I also will take into consideration some of the reported experiences of others. It would be foolish of me to argue that other forms of psychotherapy are not effective. I propose, however, that, when they are effective, it is because of the elements that I will outline in this paper. In other words, I will take on the rather daunting task of outlining the main elements which make *any* form of psychotherapy effective.

Novelty

> I create a new theory for each patient.
>
> *(Erickson, personal communication, 1977)*

"Practitioners of various forms of behavior therapy are also taking longer to obtain results" (Klein et al., 1969).

> It is hard to believe that the lengthening of treatment reflects changes in the severity of patients' problems or symptoms. More probably it reflects a decrease in therapists' zeal with the disappearance of the novelty effect, and reduction of the need to proselytize as therapy gains recognition.
>
> *(Frank, 1973)*

Several studies (Frank, 1973, p. 167) have shown that medical students obtain about the same improvement rates in short-term therapy as do psychiatrists. Certainly, the zeal that goes with novelty applies here.

Since Ericksonian therapy is now in the forefront of some people's awareness, it will take us a while to determine whether this situation prevails here. In my own experience, I have found that whenever I have tried a new approach to therapy, I would get good results at first. Curiosity, zeal, enthusiasm, novelty ... whatever it is, these are all very important factors which the therapist brings to the therapy and which are conveyed to the patient. Certainly, if, like Erickson, we approach each patient as a new challenge and create a new therapy for him, we will maintain this zeal.

Therapist Activity

> If you do not do, I will do.
>
> *(Erickson, personal communication, 1978)*

Frank (1973, p. 186) also quotes Whitehorn and Betz (Whitehorn, 1954): "More successful therapists offered a therapeutic relationship characterized by active, personal participation rather than passive permissive interpretation and instruction or practical care." In this regard Erickson's degree of active involvement in his patients' lives was rarely seen in the work of other therapists of his day. Even today, especially in psychoanalytic circles, that degree of involvement is frowned upon.

For patients who did not have the initiative or the know-how to seek out community resources, Erickson would make arrangements for them to receive help and advice in all areas, ranging from help in dressing and grooming to advice on buying genuine, high-quality turquoise ("Go to the Heard Museum"). He would accompany patients on dinner dates and arrange for the waitress to treat them in a prescribed manner. He would stage fights in order to help desensitize a patient to anger. He would do whatever was necessary to promote therapeutic or growth experiences.

Flexibility and Adaptability

Therapies may focus predominantly on the past, the present, or the future. Erickson's approaches—with age-regression, doing and experiencing on the present, and pseudo-orientation in time or age-progression—encompass all of these. Of course, if we simply use the hypnotic state in order to bring back memories from early childhood, as in hypnoanalysis, it might not be considered "Ericksonian," but on the other hand it is not prohibited within an Ericksonian framework.

Erickson was noted for developing and varying his approaches according to the existing climate and the uniqueness of the patient. In his early years, working with Lawrence Kubie, he used analytic understandings. In his later experimentation, he applied imagery and what could be called cognitive approaches. He constantly developed applications of nonverbal communication. He learned the language of psychotics, of children, of workers, and of mystics, speaking to each in their own language, even while apologizing that, "I know that I can never really understand the language of another person." He brought to his therapeutic approaches anything of value that he had learned from different areas of human knowledge—history, literature, anthropology, science, and, of course, medicine. In exploring ways of getting people to move or to change, he developed approaches which have been dubbed "strategic."

When I review the contents of a single issue of any psychotherapy journal, I am struck by many factors that might be considered the essential features which make therapy effective including production of dissociation, transference, corrective emotional experiences, and insight. Perhaps the strength of Erickson was that he did not exclude any of these, but rather included all of them and added his own innovations.

The technique of "reframing" has become identified with Erickson although other therapies also use it. Approaches which I have dubbed "corrective regression" are based on Erickson's "February Man" and are truly original; they do not seem to be included in any other therapeutic approaches. They involve the actual creation of new memories or, as somebody has put it, they prove that "it is never too late to have a happy childhood."

Erickson's own summation of "hypnosis" was that "hypnosis is the evocation and utilization of unconscious learnings" (Rosen, 1982, p. 28). As he said, "in order to do therapy, all you do is: First you model the patient's world, and then you role-model the patient's world" (Rosen, 1982, p. 35). The approaches mentioned above and dozens of others are applied within this flexible framework.

Multilevel Communication

We are all aware that a patient communicates with us on many levels. Erickson has made us more aware of the fact that we also communicate with the patient on many levels. When this communication is done with thought and intent, and when we are aware of the various ways in which we can communicate therapeutically, our results are bound to be better than if we simply rely on our desire to help, trusting that verbal interpretations, clarifications, and suggestions will be sufficient to enable us to help our patients.

A Learning Approach Rather than a Pathology Focused One

> Therapy is the substitution of a good idea for a bad idea.
> *(Erickson, personal communication, 1978)*

Erickson seemed to think of life's problems, including neuroses and psychoses, as arising from faulty or insufficient learning, or from inability to utilize the learnings which we have already acquired. The therapeutic situation gives the opportunity for new learnings and for the utilization of helpful old learnings. The therapist guides the patient, acting as a model, as a teacher, and sometimes as a guru. Learning is generally more easily achieved when the patient is in a trance state. The therapist uses the trance state in himself in order to make the best contact with the patient, and to more completely understand him. And as Minuchin stated in his letter to Erickson (Rosen, 1982, p. 18), Erickson was able "to look at simple moments and describe their complexity" and had "trust in the capacity of human beings to harness a repertory of experiences they do not know they have."

If what is learned is a result of therapeutic experiences that help the person to cope better with life, the new patterns and approaches will likely be retained and built upon so that the results will be long-lasting. They will be retained only if they can free the person to continue growing and learning.

Magic and Entering a New Reality

> Every child likes a surprise.
> *(Erickson, personal communication at the beginning of my first visit, 1970)*

When a person entered into Erickson's sphere, he entered into a new reality—a world of magic, of childhood, and of whimsical humor. In this atmosphere we are likely to revert to childlike responses, to childlike openness to learning, and to the malleability of childhood. When a therapist can create a world of wonder, of freshness of view, his patients are likely to respond with the "suggestibility" of children. Therapeutic suggestions and role modelling are bound to be more effective than they would be if presented only to the conscious, logical, "left brain" mind.

Healing has always been associated with magic, as in the healing rituals and practices of so-called "primitive" groups, or the reported practices of the temple priests in biblical times. Hypnosis has also always been associated with magic, despite efforts by Erickson and others "to disassociate the study of hypnosis from mystical and unscientific connotations" (Rosen, 1982, p. 192). In spite of our disavowals, when we do therapy under the aegis of hypnosis, we tend to arouse, in many patients, particularly the most desperate ones, overt or latent magical beliefs, and this may add power to our interventions, whether or not we ourselves believe in magic. We can benefit from the popular association between hypnosis, magic and mysticism. In scientific circles, it leads to hypnosis being viewed with scorn, but with desperate patients it adds power to our therapy and may, indeed, be one of the more powerful factors in making Ericksonian therapy "so effective."

Oracular Pronouncements, Interpretations and Directions

> You know much more than you think you know.
> Your unconscious mind will protect your conscious mind. And, at an appropriate time, in an appropriate place, your unconscious mind will let your conscious mind know something that you already know, but don't know that you know.
> *(Erickson, personal communication, 1970)*

It appears that people are most helpful to themselves when they come to their own conclusions about the causes of their problems and discover their own solutions. The wheel does seem to have to be invented over and over again. In Ericksonian therapy, this inclination is encouraged by what I call "oracular" comments, predictions and interpretations. These are statements made in ways that access the patient's inclination to look into himself to discover his own resources and his own explanations. They can be applied by almost every person to himself or herself: for example, "You have sometimes wished that your parents would die, yet you were terrified that your wish might be fulfilled" or "you have some deep-seated feelings of inadequacy."

In dealing with a patient who has premature ejaculations, I might say,

> I do not know anything about your background, your childhood, your family, your sexual history. But you know about these things. And you can, in a trance, get in touch with the things you know but don't know that you know and you can find attitudes and approaches that will enable you to enjoy sex in ways that you desire.

The patient can do his inner searching and testing of solutions more quickly alone (especially with the aid of time distortion) than he could while verbalizing his thoughts and associations. I might add, "There are certainly good reasons for your sexual responses and these good reasons will be respected, won't they?" (The implication is that invalid reasons can be ignored or overridden.)

To the above I might add, "You can find ways of changing your sexual response so that you are able to achieve and give much more satisfaction than you have been able to up to this time." Evaluation of "how much is much?" is very subjective, of course. In other words, it will be done, again, according to the patient's needs and in keeping with his values, goals and understandings.

These types of statements, including truisms, "pacing" and an invitation for an inner search, are similar to the pronouncements at the Oracle of Delphi in that they are interpreted by each listener according to his own needs and understandings.

Encouraging a Minimal Change

> Therapy is like starting a snowball rolling down a mountain. It builds up momentum and it can grow into an avalanche and all the therapist has to do is start the snowball rolling.
>
> *(Erickson, personal communication, 1978)*

It has been noted that hypnotic subjects want to please the hypnotist. Paradoxically, with open-ended suggestions and directions, the patient can best please by pleasing himself, perhaps by interpreting his future responses so as to confirm the therapist's expectation that the patient can solve his own problem. He may also interpret his future responses so as to produce a positive effect of the therapist's open-ended, generalized "oracular" statements. Subsequently, he will have the feeling that he is making progress. This feeling of success leads to increased confidence, to a readiness to take risks, which may lead to still further progress, and so on.

As a patient is encouraged to value minimal changes, he is likely to expect to make further changes. At least the readiness to change and explore and experiment is increased when some changes, even minimal ones, are recognized.

Altered States of Consciousness

> Hypnosis is the evocation and the utilization of unconscious learnings.
>
> *(Rosen, 1982, p. 28)*

Intrapsychically

If we examine all psychotherapies, we find that change is most likely to be initiated when the patient is in an altered state of consciousness. Some might even say that all healing is promoted with alterations in consciousness. Doctors have traditionally prescribed rest or a voyage or a change of scene for many chronic ailments. Medications such as hypnotics and tranquilizers, group experiences leading to emotional abreactions, sleep cures and activity cures, all lead to alterations of the patients' usual states of consciousness.

Simply helping a patient to enter into a state of consciousness which is different from that in which he is symptomatic may alleviate the symptoms or the disturbed mode of functioning. Rossi, in his outline of the stages of hypnotic induction, points out that the second stage is the interruption and depotentiation of the patient's usual mental sets (Erickson & Rossi, 1979). This depotentiation may apply not only to the set at the moment but also, with post-hypnotic suggestions, to the patient's "symptomatic mental set" which may be associated with compulsions, anxiety, depression, and so on. Thus, trance inductions, per se, may be very helpful for many patients.

The next stage of hypnotic induction—the "inner search," with or without guidance from the therapist—may lead to more specific therapeutic changes. Thus, on an intrapsychic level, the use of trance may expedite therapy.

Interpersonally

Contact between therapist and patient, which may lead to the patient's increased capacity to establish and maintain better contact with friends and intimates, is widely understood to be an important element in psychotherapy. It is often discussed under the rubric of "therapist-patient" relationship. In approaches such as Gestalt therapy it is specifically emphasized. Martin Buber has stated that it is only man with man who can be fulfilled or it is only in an "I-Thou" relationship that growth can occur. In other words, it is only in close or intimate relationship with others that one can grow. The therapeutic relationship should be one of these.

The trance state involves one of the most intimate relationships. In fact, in the trance state the barrier between the hypnotist and the subject is broken down and to some extent may even be eliminated. The subject then experiences the hypnotist's voice as coming from inside himself. In other words, it sounds and feels like his own voice. Obviously, the patient will not necessarily follow even his own inner vocalizations all the time, but they are certainly more influential than the voices of others.

In the trance state there really appears to be communication with the "unconscious mind" of the patient, communication on the deepest levels. As a result, the patient is most receptive to therapeutic interventions, whether they be strategic prescriptions, role modelling, indirect suggestions, behavioral instructions, or cognitive restructuring.

Change of Self-Concept

> All successful therapies implicitly or explicitly change the patient's image of himself, as a person who is overwhelmed by his symptoms and problems to that of one who can master them.
>
> *(Frank, 1973, p. 330)*

Techniques such as self-hypnosis promote this sense of mastery directly. The patient will no longer feel so overwhelmed by anxieties, by phobias, by his limitations. Changing "inner scripts" and "inner dialogues" can be accomplished most effectively when the patient is in a trance state. Ego boosting suggestions are routinely used.

"All forms of psychotherapy help the patient overcome his sense of alienation from his fellows" (Frank, 1973). In Ericksonian therapy this is especially likely to happen when patients are seen in a group, as in Erickson's teaching seminars. Here the element of commonly shared experiences and being able to relate more closely to one another was more likely to be experienced, particularly with the breaking down of barriers that occurs when people are in a hypnotic trance together.

Experience Counts

> You don't learn to do psychotherapy from books. You learn from experience.
> *(Erickson, personal communication, 1978)*

Our patients also learn to live from experience. Since the 1960s, the trend in psychotherapy has been to emphasize experiencing rather than insight. As Fromm-Reichmann said, "Patients need experiences, not explanations."[2] Ericksonian approaches make experiencing, often with heightened emotions, more likely to happen than with the more intellectually oriented approaches. With a focusing of attention on them in a trance state, experiences in the therapeutic session are apt to be more vivid, whether they be a heightened awareness of present perceptions, thoughts and emotions or a "reliving," even in fantasy, of past experiences.

I have seen many patients who have undergone years of psychoanalysis or psychoanalytically-oriented psychotherapy and who have told me that they had never really experienced some early memories before doing so in a trance state. My own personal experience with Erickson confirms this. Having an intense or dramatic experience, particularly one that has not been experienced before, is a real "convincer" of the power of the therapy. And the broadening of experiencing in the therapeutic session often makes possible a parallel, or even extended, broadening of experiencing in life.

In the dedication of his book, *The Language of Change*, Paul Watzlawick (1978) paid tribute "to Milton H. Erickson who heals with words." Elsewhere, Watzlawick (1982) writes,

> What he taught us above all was a different use of language. Traditionally, the language of therapy is the language of interpretation, explanation, clarification and the like. It is an explanatory language and must be so because it stands in the service of consciousness-raising. By contrast, the language of

hypnosis is injunctive, because its ultimate message, no matter how carefully veiled, is "*Do* something!"

(p. 149)

Explanations and Pseudo-Explanations

Any acceptable explanation can relieve anxiety and promote hope. This is probably the way "insight" helps in most psychotherapies. Sometimes it is difficult to differentiate between a "true" explanation and a pseudo-explanation and from the point of view of the patient it seems to make little difference, at least for the purpose of relieving anxiety.

Watzlawick has pointed out the therapeutic value of naming a patient's condition. (Physicians call it diagnosing.) He quotes Gordon Allport's story of a dying patient to illustrate this. The patient had been informed that the physicians could not diagnose his condition. A bit of hope was held that a famous visiting specialist might have more luck. The visitor did not even pause at the poor patient's bedside. He simply strode past and proclaimed "moribundus"—on the verge of death. After hearing this "diagnosis" the patient made a rapid and complete recovery (Watzlawick, 1985).

If we reframe a situation into one which augments a patient's sense of worth instead of diminishing it (positive reframing), we are going a step further. For example, I am doing this if I tell a patient with premature ejaculation that he is suffering not from a lack of sexual strength, but from too much sexual energy. I am renaming his "premature ejaculation" as "excess sexual drive." Subsequently, we do not need to spend weeks or years in "uncovering" the "causes" of this "ailment." Instead, we can teach him to direct and control this energy—a much easier and quicker process.

Suggestion

Freud's fear that someday the pure gold of psychoanalysis would be polluted by the lead of suggestion was unwarranted. The "pollution" had already occurred! Expectations of the patient and therapist and suggestion are powerful elements in all psychotherapies, including psychoanalysis. In Ericksonian psychotherapy these elements are emphasized explicitly. Thus, our concern is not whether or not we will use suggestion, but to what end that suggestion is to be directed. What are the goals and values that the therapist is promoting and encouraging? Or, what goals do the therapist and patient evolve together?

Suggestions can be thought of as coming primarily from the patient (autosuggestions) or from the therapist (heterosuggestions).

Autosuggestions

These are generated by the patient's expectations, values, beliefs, inner images, scripts, and inner dialogues, all of which contribute to the patient's self-concept and emanate from it. As Paracelsus said, "Even as man imagines himself to be, such he is, and he is also that which he imagines" (Damon, 1971, p. 322).

Values, beliefs and life scripts may be thought of as long-term autosuggestions. They may also apply on a short-term basis. Erickson told a story (Rossi, Ryan, & Sharpe, 1983) in which he described a patient at the Colorado Psychopathic Hospital who had announced, "I'm going to die next Saturday morning. I am dying on Saturday at 10 o'clock in the morning, on such and such a date." He said the man slept well and ate well. His blood pressure was fine. His blood chemistry was fine. Every index in his physical examination was fine. Saturday morning, we all gathered around and watched that patient die at 10 o'clock. The autopsy showed no reason whatsoever for the patient's death. Erickson's conclusion was, "It shows the effects of thoughts and feelings and attitudes and beliefs on the functioning of the human body. (These same mechanisms are the ones you try to direct and utilize in a positive way in hypnosis)" (Rossi, Ryan, & Sharpe, 1983, p. 180).

Working with patients on the deepest levels, such as the level of beliefs, may often make it unnecessary to deal with specific areas of their lives or with symptoms. Altering the roots or the foundation may lead to proliferation of the newer, healthier structures to the branches.

Heterosuggestions

These include the expectations and suggestions, direct and indirect, of the therapist. As we can clearly see now, psychoanalysis, along with all other psychotherapies, has, from its beginning, derived many of its successes largely from suggestion. The power of suggestions is heightened by the intense "positive transference" or "rapport" which is associated with a trance state. Psychoanalytic patients enter into a trance state as the result of undergoing the process of inner searching and free associating, while in the state of sensory deprivation, which characterizes the psychoanalytic situation. In fact, psychoanalysis is really a slower form of hypnotic therapy.

By hypnotic therapy I mean a therapy which aims at changing behavior, thinking and responses which we consider "unconscious." By "unconscious" I refer to parts of the mind which may, under certain circumstances, be dissociated from consciousness. And Erickson's definition, "Hypnosis is the evocation and the utilization of unconscious learnings" (Rosen, 1982, p. 28), applies equally well to psychoanalysis. It is slower, that's all. And, sometimes, it may be better to be slower.

Psychoanalysts expect that if their patients can come up with and then "work through" "repressed material" they will get better. When these expectations are met, the patients are likely to value themselves more highly and have the courage to venture into other new behavior. Erickson also had expectations of his patients. When asked, "Why do patients do the crazy things you ask?" his answer once was, "Because I expect them to" (personal communication, 1978). He not only expected them to do as he asked, but he asked them to do things, such as surpassing their previous limitations, which would insure their getting well.

Working with his guidance, we therapists have more options than those allowed by any one "school" of therapy. Our patients also have more options. They can "get better" (I'm using this simple phrase to include relief of symptoms, overcoming of limitations, growth, capacity to cope) as a result of abreaction, relearning, self-understanding, imaging, carrying on new inner dialogues, or changing inner scripts. They can get better by going beyond their previous restrictions in behavior and thinking and feeling. And this transcendence of previous limitations may be engineered by the therapist with strategies which make it possible for new experiencing to occur.

I agree with Hammond (1984) that too much emphasis has been placed on Erickson's use of confusion techniques and of indirect suggestion. In most cases, it is probable that clear-cut direct suggestions and guidance are most appropriate and most effective. But, as Zeig (1980) has noted, "The amount of indirection necessary is directly proportional to the perceived resistance" (p. 25). The planning and use of interspersed suggestions, anecdotes, and word plays may make these suggestions more acceptable to some patients, but, as Erickson pointed out, they add to the "elegance" of the treatment, thus making the doing of therapy more interesting and more fun for the therapist and patient. Patients benefit more from being with a therapist who enjoys his work than with one who is bored.

Goals of the Therapist

Erickson's goals or expectations for his patients were that they would achieve a greater sense of mastery in their own lives, a sense of optimism, an ability to live in the present while relating well to others and contributing to the welfare of others.

Another way of outlining the goals of Ericksonian psychotherapy is that they are aimed at helping us achieve a sense of comfort, mastery and self-worth.

What is Patient Cured From? What is He Cured To?

We may not be able to compete with faith healers, gurus and quacks in terms of numbers. Hopefully we can offer better or healthier possibilities of growth, self-fulfillment and contributions to society. In order to do this, however, we must be cognizant of our own values and, like Erickson, strive toward expanding our own learning, growth and social contributions. "We all have our limitations," Erickson said. "We have to discover what those limitations really are" (personal communication, 1978).

Humor

> Spread humor knee deep everywhere.
>
> *(Erickson, personal communication, 1980)*

The healing power of humor has been recognized more and more in recent years. Obviously, it helps us and our patients when we can put things into perspective. We need to see the patient's dilemmas and our own problems in the light of the ultimate absurdities and with knowledge of the pitifully short time that we have in which to enjoy our life and fulfill some purpose. The distance that one needs in order to view systems is most easily achieved when we adopt a humorous or whimsical stance. And, with the feeling that everything is not necessarily a matter of life and death, we and, by example, our patients may have the courage to take the risks and make the changes that, as Shakespeare pointed out in Hamlet's soliloquy, we are so loath to do.

Conclusion

As I was finishing writing this chapter, my daughter hypnotized me and suggested that I follow the above advice and take a lighter view of the opus that I have just presented to you. In my trance I saw a bunch of people serving themselves from a smorgasbord. So, here it is. Serve yourself. Take what is useful to you. Chew on it; add your own spices and condiments to your taste. Digest it well and eliminate any excesses or irrelevancies.

Notes

1 This chapter was previously published in *Developing Ericksonian Therapy: State of the Art*, 1988, edited by Jeffrey Zeig and Stephen R. Lankton, as Chapter 1, pp. 5–21.
2 Quoted by Rollo May at The Evolution of Psychotherapy Conference, December, 1985, Phoenix, Ariz.

References

Damon, S.F. (1971). *A Blake Dictionary: The Ideas and Symbols of William Blake*. New York: Dutton.
Erickson, M.H., and Rossi, E.L. (1979). *Hypnotherapy: An Exploratory Casebook*. New York: Irvington.
Erickson, M.H., Rossi, E.L., and Ryan, M. O. (eds) (1984). *Life Reframing in Hypnosis*. New York: Irvington.
Frank, J. (1973). *Persuasion and Healing*. Baltimore: Johns Hopkins U. Press.
Hammond, D.C. (1984, April). Myths about Erickson and Ericksonian hypnosis. *American Journal of Clinical Hypnosis*, 26(4): 236–245.
Heine, R.W. (ed.) (1962). *The Student Physician as Psychotherapist*. Chicago: Univ. of Chicago Press.
Hoffman, E. (1981). *The Way of Splendour*. Boulder: Shambala Publications.
Klein, M.H., Dittman, A.T., Parloff, M.R., and Gill, M.W. (1969). Behavior therapy: Observations and reflections. *Journal Consulting and Clinical Psychology*, 33(3): 259–266.
Lindsey, R. (1986). Teachings of "Ramtha" Draw Hundreds West. *New York Times*, Nov. 16, page 1.

Rosen, S. (ed.) (1982). *My Voice Will Go With You: The Teaching Tales of Milton H. Erickson, M.D.* New York: W. W. Norton.

Rossi, E.L., Ryan, M.O., and Sharpe, F.A. (eds) (1983). *Healing in Hypnosis.* New York: Irvington.

Turnbull, C. (1983). *The Human Cycle.* New York: Simon & Schuster.

Uhlenhuth, E.H., and Duncan, D.B. (1968). Subjective Change With Medical Student Therapist: Some Determinants Of Change In Psychoneurotic Outpatients. *Archives of General Psychiatry*, 18(5): 532–540.

Watzlawick, P. (1978). *The Language of Change.* New York: Basic Books.

Watzlawick, P. (1982). Erickson's Contribution to the Interactional View of Psychotherapy. In J.K. Zeig (ed.), *Ericksonian Approaches to Hypnosis and Psychotherapy*, pp. 147–154. New York: Brunner/Mazel.

Watzlawick, P. (1985). Hypnotherapy without trance. In J.K. Zeig (ed.), *Ericksonian Psychotherapy Vol. 1: Structures*, pp. 5–14. New York: Brunner/Mazel.

Whitehorn, J.C., and Betz, B.J. (1954). A study of psychotherapeutic relationships between physicians and schizophrenic patients. *American Journal of Psychiatry*, 111(5): 321–331.

Zeig, J.K. (ed.) (1980). *A Teaching Seminar with Milton H. Erickson, M.D.*, New York: Brunner/Mazel.

3

ONE THOUSAND INDUCTION TECHNIQUES AND THEIR APPLICATION TO THERAPY AND THINKING[1]

Introduction

Anytime a person focuses on one thing, he or she will go into a trance. Others have identified focusing on something as a prerequisite to going into a trance. I go a step further. In my view, simply by focusing on something you'll go into a trance. It's not a step; it's the main approach, which makes a person more likely to become open to suggestion. In this chapter, I test out the hypothesis in different situations. For example, in a group where everyone receives a suggestion of focusing on a smell or sound, everyone in the group showed signs that indicated the presence of a trance state.

In his introduction to *Hypnotherapy: An Exploratory Casebook* (Erickson & Rossi, 1979), Ernest Rossi indicated that he believed that the utilization approach and indirect forms of suggestion were the essence of Erickson's therapeutic innovations: "We now believe that the utilization approach and the indirect forms of suggestions are the essence of the senior author's therapeutic innovations over the past fifty years and account for much of his unique skill as a hypnotherapist" (p. xiv). That was Rossi's summation of the essence of Erickson's hypnotic therapy.

In his discussion of the therapeutic trance state, Rossi describes stages ranging from "the fixation of attention" to "depotentiating habitual frameworks and belief systems." He elaborates various elements to bring out these stages, for example: "distraction, shock, surprise, doubt, confusion, dissociation, or any other process that interrupts the patient's habitual frameworks."

I would add that focusing on one thing, which obviously interrupts the patient's habitual frameworks, is way of directing attention, inducing a state of suggestibility. So many therapeutic and spiritual activities—from acupuncture and meditation to gestalt—all involve focusing attention on one thing. But they also can lead to a particular way of focusing.

For example, acupuncture is connected with suggestions that the installation of the needles leads to a therapeutic response. For crystal healing, you just hold the crystal over a certain area and that draws attention to that area, focusing attention on one thing, on the sensation that one experiences, and the ideas connected with those sensations.

Once one experiences the sensations that come from focusing attention, then one is more likely to accept other suggestions, such as relaxation or diminution of pain. Putting it another way, when you're focused on one thing, the usual mental activity of the mind is left in the background. Our minds are almost always operating on many different levels, and once we push those different levels to the background, other thoughts and distractions are also eliminated or lessened. As a result, suggestions presented in the foreground are most likely to be effective.

Erickson said that therapy consists of substituting a good idea for a bad idea. Once a person is in a receptive state, the "good ideas" that Erickson encouraged have an effect on the person's reactions and interpretations of mental thoughts and ideas.

Shamans, healers, and psychotherapists can use this power of imagination. And people can engage in self-hypnosis to change their own imaginative self-conceptions. What the therapist tries to do is to utilize some manifestations that we may not have been aware of and evoke other responses that turn out to be therapeutic. The substitution of bad ideas for good ones involves the technique of switching.

Paracelsus, too, emphasized the power of the imagination to change reality, insisting that "As a man imagines himself to be, so shall he be, and he is that which he imagines." In this chapter, I emphasize the power of imagination and imagery to change and direct one's experience. The emphasis is directed away from conscious control, or willpower—that is, when you're working hard to make something happen—and toward the utilization of the powerful effects of suggestions and imagery. The power of the imagination doesn't have to be experienced consciously. It's not something that can be affected through willpower. (Imagination may affect willpower but willpower doesn't necessarily change our unconscious patterns). In fact, the attempt to change pain or anxiety by the use of consciousness willpower often evokes the opposite response: the more you try to get rid of their pain, the more you feel it.

The attempts to get rid of pain require that you concentrate on the pain, and conscious concentration on the pain causes the intensification of the experience. I also emphasize in this chapter that it is not necessary to evoke an experience in an altered state of consciousness. Simply having suggestions given in a strong—or even quiet—authoritative voice in a particular setting may be even more effective than when a person feels that he or she is in a trance.

★★★

The Nature of a Hypnotic Trance

I do not need to stress that a trance is not a state of being asleep, unconscious, or "under." It need not involve relaxation, even though most of us use it at some time or other to help elicit relaxation.

Trance is a state of hypersuggestibility. A person in hypnosis tends to be more responsive than usual to suggestions or influence from a hypnotist or, with self-hypnosis, from himself or herself. The latter includes expectations and "self-talk." If the suggestions are designed to focus attention, it will then tend to be focused on a designated object or mode of experiencing or thinking. And, of course, in a trance one can be more in touch than usual with what we call the Unconscious Mind. In fact, Erickson's last definition of hypnosis was that "hypnosis is the evocation and utilization of unconscious learnings" (personal communication, 1978).

Hypnosis can make possible intense communication between people, communication on more levels than usual. Many have had the experience, when in a trance while working therapeutically, of responding to our patient's mood and thoughts even before they were verbalized. It seemed like mind reading, but undoubtedly came from increased sensitivity and increased recollection of past patterns of thinking, as well as an increased awareness of minimal sensory and bodily cues. And the patient, of course, was then most responsive to our suggestions and influence. Increased responsiveness occurs when attention is directed almost exclusively toward the patient not when we are in a more self-centered state of mind.

People are not more hypnotizable because they are more suggestible. They become more suggestible when they are in a trance. About 25 years ago, I heard Lawrence Kubie, the well-known psychoanalyst who wrote three papers with Erickson, discuss hypnosis at a meeting of the American Psychoanalytic Association. He pointed out that people will go into trance under many conditions, without any suggestions having been given—watching the line on the highway, listening to a repeated tone, being stroked repeatedly on the forehead or on the back. Kubie noted that after the person goes into a trance, the barrier between the hypnotist and the subject is dissolved and the subject hears the hypnotist's voice as if it were coming from inside his or her own head. That is why the hypnotized subject is more suggestible and also why he does not necessarily follow all suggestions that are given, just as he does not act on all of his own thoughts.

How, then, can we enter, or help someone else enter, into a trance? From the examples I have mentioned, we know that we can do this by utilizing a repeated stimulus—visual, auditory, or tactile. For many years, hypnotists relied on repetition, but one of the early contributions that Erickson made to hypnotherapy was his demonstrating that it was unnecessary to repeat suggestions. In fact, casual seeding of a suggestion may be most effective.

In contemplating this question a few years ago, I made a rather large leap. I have always thought that it came from reading a comment by John Beahrs in

Erickson's 75th birthday issue of the *American Journal of Clinical Hypnosis* (Vol. 20, 1977). I clearly remembered that Beahrs had written, "Anytime a person focuses attention on one thing he will go into a trance." I have credited Dr. Beahrs with this insight. In preparing this chapter, however, all efforts to find this quotation failed. In desperation, I called John and asked where he had made this statement. He could not remember ever having said exactly that. The closest he could recall was a comment in an article he wrote with Humiston in which he stated:

> It is our experience that whenever a patient is successfully held to vivid experience of whatever is happening anyway, the patient invariably goes into a hypnotic trance.... This is evidenced by vivid real-life imagery, profound body image experiences, and time distortion, all recognized by Hilgard (Hilgard, 1968) as bona-fide criteria of hypnosis.
> *(Beahrs & Humiston, 1972, p. 2)*

It appears, then, that I had either extrapolated and expanded on this observation, simply misinterpreted it, or read something somewhere else. In any case, I had concluded, from my experience, that *anytime a person focuses on one thing he or she will go into a trance.*

I have tested this hypothesis in many different settings—in my office with patients, in seminars with therapists, and, of course, with myself—and it seems to be supported. For example, I may suggest to a group of people that they touch something and focus on the sensation of touch; that they look at something and focus on the image, that they recall a smell such as the smell of cut lemon or apple, that they make a sound and focus on listening to the sound, that they visualize the number 687, a color, or their own first name. Within 80 seconds, almost everyone in the group shows signs that we recognize as indicating the presence of a trance state—e.g., facial lines smooth out, the body becomes immobile, eyelids close, or the eyes assume a staring condition. When, at this point I suggest, "Now you can go into as deep a trance as you want and utilize your trance—for some useful purpose," or "utilize your trance to recall a long-forgotten childhood memory," or "utilize your trance to feel more relaxed than you have felt for a long time," a large number of participants are able to follow the suggestion I have presented. In other words, they go into a trance and become more suggestible or more responsive than usual.

I have divided an audience into four groups:

Group One was instructed to fix their eyes on any point or object. When, within 30 seconds, most of them gave evidence of being in a trance—flattened facial expressions, eyes closed or staring, immobility, with or without relaxed musculature, slowing in breathing—they were told, "Now, you can go into as deep a trance as you like and take yourself to a beautiful vacation spot."

Group Two was invited to take objects from their pockets or purses and to concentrate on feeling the texture and shape of the objects. When they appeared to be in a trance, they were—told, "Now, you can go into as deep a trance as you want—and enjoy a feeling of deep calm and peace."

Group Three was advised to listen to an imagined or recalled sound. It was suggested to them that they could then smell and taste a freshly sliced apple.

Group Four were directed to visualize and think of the number "637." They were told to bring back an early memory that they had not thought of for a long time. When asked for a show of hands afterward to indicate that they had felt themselves to be in a trance, 60% to 75% of each group responded positively. Approximately the same percentages indicated that they had successfully experienced the suggested phenomena.

Of course, once we had demonstrated the effectiveness of the "637" induction technique, we had paved the way for the "688" technique, the "5,294" technique and so on. If we include the objects of all of our senses—tactile, olfactory, hearing, and vision—the number of objects of focus is truly limitless.

> Question: What do the following activities have in common, acupuncture, shiatsu, zone therapy, crystal healing, psychoanalysis, meditation, the "awareness continuum-exercise" of Gestalt therapy, Eye Movement Desensitization and Reprocessing (EMDR), Benson's "Relaxation Response" and hypnosis?
>
> Answer: They are modalities in which, by focusing attention on one thing at a time, a person can move into a receptive state in which he or she is most open to suggestions of healing and learning (perhaps to other suggestions, as well). As I have indicated, I call this a trance state.

In acupuncture and shiatsu, the attention is drawn to points that are touched. In zone therapy, the attention is drawn to pressure sensations on the bottom of the foot. With crystal healing, it is directed toward seeing the sparkling or colored crystal and feeling the kinesthetic sensations that one becomes aware of when paying attention to the parts of the body that are touched or approached by the crystal. In psychoanalysis the attention is drawn to the subject's thoughts and feelings; these inner mental experiences constitute the "one thing" upon which attention is focused. In meditation practices, the attention is focused on a mantra, as the sound "OM". It may be focused on a visual pattern, called a "yantra" in Tantric practices, or it may be focused on breathing or on the thinking processes themselves. In Eye Movement Desensitization and Reprocessing (EMDR), it is directed toward the feelings in the muscles that accompany lateral eye movements. And, in order to evoke the "Relaxation Response," one need only concentrate on one thing, the number "one."

I do not mean to imply that any of the practices I have mentioned or that any of the other New Age healing approaches are "just hypnosis." I am simply pointing out that they all involve the evocation and utilization of a receptive state, which can be designated as a trance or a hypnotic state. The nature and quality of that state depends to a great extent on the input presented to the subject. This input may come from the outside, as from "demand characteristics of the situation" (Orne, 1962) and from verbal and nonverbal suggestions. It may come from another person or even from a computer screen. Or it may come from the subject's own mind, in the form of self-suggestions and expectations. For example, if the subject is seeking a state of transcendence, she is likely to identify trance experiences of dissociation as being transcendental. If the suggestion is made, or the expectation (self-suggestion) exists, that healing "will occur, it is more likely to happen." If the suggestion is made that the subject will be in touch with his "unconscious mind," he will respond with appropriate images, memories, and behaviors.

To summarize: the receptive state is initiated by the subjects being directed and aided toward focusing attention on one thing—such as the sensations on the bottom of the foot, eye movements, "free associations," or a mantra. In this state, suggestions will be followed so long as they are ego syntonic, that is, in keeping with the subject's values and goals.

Early Learning Set Induction

Focusing is clearly illustrated in Erickson's Early Learning Set Induction, (Personal communication, 1978). In this, as in other inductions every step involves focusing on, one thing at a time. Following Erickson, I begin with,

> I'd like to remind you that many of the things you now do automatically, once required conscious mental effort. For example, you don't remember how you first learned to read and write, but just to tell the difference between the letter "a" and the letter "o" was a difficult task ... and how do you put together a straight line and a little circle to form a "b" or a "d" or a "p" or a "q", and are there two bumps on the "m" and three on the "n" or are there two bumps on the "n" and, three on the "m"?

Wondering whether or not these statements are true and trying to visualize all of these, suggested letters, even if unsuccessfully, leads to a focusing of attention—on the lines, circles, and resulting letters, on the concept of putting together the lines and circles, or even on the failure to see letters.

The induction continues:

> Do you dot the "t" and cross the "i" or do you dot the "i" and cross the "t"? ... And what made it even more difficult was that there were small letters and capital letters. There were written letters and printed letters.

After the subject has entered into a trance by focusing attention on the suggested items, he or she is more "suggestible" than usual and is therefore more likely to respond to subsequent suggestions. First, he is given the reinforcing and reassuring reminder:

> And you learned to write all of those letters ... you learned to write them automatically. And there are so many things you do automatically. You walk automatically. You talk automatically. You count four fingers, two thumbs automatically.

Then comes the suggestion:

> And you can go into a trance automatically ... simply by letting your eyelids close ... the next time I say the word, "now." Let your eyelids close nowwww.

I will usually continue with further direction to focus on one thing at a time. For example:

> And with your eyes closed; you can examine your eyelids. You may see shadows. You may see some light here or there. You may see patterns and lines. You may see some colors.... But it really doesn't matter whether or not you see anything at all. Because the important thing is that you are again focusing attention on one thing ... on your eyelids.

For deepening of the trance, I may suggest:

> If you would like to go deeper into your trance, keep close track of any phenomenon that interests you, anything that is in the forefront of your consciousness, and your curiosity will draw you deeper and deeper into your trance.

Obviously that last direction, similar to the Awareness Continuum Exercise of Gestalt therapy, again directs the subject to continue focusing on one thing at a time and it is certainly most easy to focus on a phenomenon that interests you, isn't it?

By this time you may be wondering, as I have, whether or not it might be useful to define our experiences so as to state that we are frequently in some kind of trance. We can talk about being in a "Lovemaking trance," a "Working trance," an "Instrument-playing Trance," a "Therapist Trance," a "Problem-solving Trance." We can be in a "Bird-watching Trance," a "Tennis-playing Trance," or a "Reading Trance." Whenever we are concentrating our-attention and energies in one area of functioning, we could define our state as being a trance.

However, since there has been a tradition of associating the word "trance" with unusual states of consciousness, it would probably be best for me to substitute a term such as "state of mind" for trance. For the rest of this chapter, I will use the terms "trance" and "'state of mind" or "state'" interchangeably.

Imagination and Imagery

Erickson suggested to me one day that "therapy consists of substituting a good idea for a bad idea." The ability to do this would obviously be helpful not only for therapy but also for better thinking. Let us consider therapy first. It is a bad idea to anticipate panic and pain. It is a good idea to expect comfort and pleasure while flying in a plane or while eating in a restaurant. But how can one change a negative or symptomatic response to a positive or comfortable one? The answer to that question can be found by a review of the literature of the healing arts, including the approaches and techniques devised and used by those who practice hypnotherapy. I cannot summarize this vast amount of information, but I can point out a basic principle. It is expressed by the dictum of Paracelsus, the physician and alchemist of the early sixteenth century: "Even as man imagines himself to be, such he is, and he is also that which he imagines" (Damon, 1971).

This same power of imagery and imagination was inadvertently confirmed by the French commission that examined the work of Mesmer and reported, after observing his follower, D'Eslon that they could find no evidence of magnetism, but that many of the patients appeared to benefit from the ministrations; this benefit, they postulated, was merely due to their imagination.

While they, like most modern-day thinkers, used the term "imagination" with negative connotations, others, following William Blake, who was himself influenced by Paracelsus, have been able to recognize the central importance of imagination and imagery in our experiencing and responding. Blake, in fact, placed the imagination above our ordinary life and existence in our world, which he called the "Vegetable Universe." "In your own Bosom you bear your Heaven and Earth and all you behold; tho'it appear Without, it is Within, in your Imagination, of which this World of Mortality is but a Shadow" (Keynes, 1969, p. 709).

Imagery and imagination are most obviously utilized by shamans and psychotherapists. We have psychotherapeutic approaches that are aimed at altering the general images that patients hold of themselves. These include approaches aimed at freeing the "hero" or the "child" within and those that center around projections into the future. Other psychotherapeutic approaches may be focused on changing a discrete area of a person functioning—eliminating a specific symptom or area of dysfunction, such as a phobia.

Switches

Images, like other mental inputs such as colors and words, tone of voice, spatial perceptions, smells, or touch sensations, can be utilized as "switches" so that focusing attention on them will evoke a particular state of mind. If this state is a desired one, we could call it a positive state, and the switch could be called a positive switch. For example, I had a patient who was suffering from excruciating, intractable lower back pain with a condition that neurosurgeons had determined was inoperable. We discovered that when she could enter into a trance and recall the feeling of holding her newborn infant, a child who was now over 40 years old, her pain would disappear. The visual and tactile memories could be called positive switches.

If the state is not desired—e.g. a negative state, such as a phobic panic state—we can identify the negative switch or switches that evoke it. The most obvious and direct negative switches are the phobic objects or situation themselves—mice or small spaces, for example. Or the thought, "I shouldn't smoke" or "I shouldn't eat dessert" will evoke the compulsive need to smoke or overeat. Negative switches are often easy to identify in phobias anxiety reactions and depressive reactions as well as in the bodily responses that we call "psychosomatic."

A switch need not include an entire scene, or sentence. Often one element or one word can evoke a desired response. Colors, tactile memories, or memories of body positions associated with successful performances have been used successfully with athletes, for example.

To change negative responses, we can use different switches—e.g., with flying phobia, we can teach a person to focus attention on his eyelids or on the weight of his hands. This practice can become associated with feelings of comfort, even of pleasure, and this response can supersede the previous panic reaction. Or we can change the response to existing switches—e.g., change panic response to a needle to a comfort response. We have many approaches for doing this, including desensitization and the introduction of other associations. These can result in the substitution of a positive trance for a negative trance. Thus, instead of, "Whenever I think of food, I am compelled to eat," one can substitute, "Whenever I think of food, I can remind myself that I have had enough. I can remind myself that my mind needs feeding and then can seek some way to feed my mind."

Instead of the panic state that is switched on with inner suggestions such as, "Whenever I move more than one block away from home I will go into a panic," one can substitute, "I can thank my body for letting me know that I am anxious, that I am moving too quickly, too slowly, or whatever. And I can move at my own pace."

These latter directions could be thought of as post-hypnotic suggestions that will be evoked by the switch of "Whenever …"

First Conscious then Automatic

While we can determine or control our entry into certain states of mind, simply, with self-hypnotic exercises, we may require more complex preparations for others. They may require an "entry process." For example, in order to enter into a "lovemaking state," many people must first proceed through some initiatory procedures or, even rituals. In order to enter into some states—a speech-making state, for example—some people will go through weeks of preparation, thinking, gathering notes, writing out the speech, practicing its delivery, composing cue cards, going through a period of anticipatory anxiety or stage fright, and finally entering into the optimal state for delivery of the speech.

In order to be able to go into a "doctor state," "a healer state," or a "therapist state," all of us had to go through years of schooling, training, and experience. Otherwise, we could probably, like actors, play the role but not be the "genuine article." We would know it and some of the people we tried to fool would also know it. But even after developing the skills, we are not always in the "therapist state," naive cocktail party acquaintances expectations to the contrary. We enter the "state" only under particular circumstances—in our offices, when we are asked for help. Outside circumstances or requests of others, therefore, play large part in evoking the "state."

I am interested in the relationship between outside stimuli and response states. As therapists, we consciously and often unconsciously use words, tone of voice, body posture, and other nonverbal communications as switches—to evoke feelings of security and comfort in our patients, for example. We can also help them and ourselves to find and discover the environments that are most conducive to their healthy functioning. But I am even more interested in helping people to determine their own inner responses—emotionally, cognitively, and even behaviorally—independently of outside stimuli. It has been said that we cannot always control or determine what happens in our lives, but we can determine our responses, our way of looking at what happens, our emotional reactions. I know that most of the time we do not make any effort to do this. In fact, most of the time we react in some habitual or even conditioned way. But we *can* determine our responses. And you will naturally ask, "How?"

My answer is: by entering into the kind of state that we choose. Not, necessarily the one that we learned to enter into during our long period of childhood hypnosis. Then we can ask our unconscious for direction. This direction will come from our "inner learnings."

For example, if our feelings are hurt by someone's slight or omission, we can learn to follow Erickson's suggestion, "Don't hold on to hurt feelings. Throw them into the nearest garbage can and take a bath" (personal communication, 1980). Now, for some of us, perhaps those who had direct contact with Erickson and especially those who were told this by him, just the recollection of his words may be enough to take us out of our "hurt feelings state" and enable us to move to the "cleansed post-bath state." Others might need to go through a short or longer period of self-hypnosis during which they would eliminate the hurt feeling, perhaps by utilizing imagery in which those feelings are sent into the stratosphere via a helium filled balloon. Then, still in a self-induced trance, they could suggest to themselves that they can find another, nonhurting way of framing or filtering the situation that led to the hurt or angry feelings. I am not suggesting that this process is always easy, but if we recall Erickson's observation, "Many of the things that we now do automatically once required conscious mental effort," then we will do the mental practicing that is required to develop needed abilities.

I will remind you that we can always enter into a receptive trance state by focusing attention on one thing at a time. But how do we get others, or our self, to focus attention on one thing? We may simply ask them to do so or we may order them, challenge them, intrigue them or even suggest that they try not to do so—e.g., "Try not to think of the word 'elephant.'" We may utilize shock, humor, confusion, questions—all the elements that Erickson and Rossi have listed in *Hypnotherapy: An Exploratory Casebook* (Erickson & Rossi, 1979). But, as I have already mentioned, one of the best ways is to instruct them to keep close track of any phenomenon that interests them.

Trance in Psychotherapy

As I have noted, all the interventions in all forms of psychotherapy (and in many healing approaches that are not universally considered to be psychotherapy) are most effective when the patient is in trance, which we might call a "receptiveness-to-healing state." Even though this is not the only element in psychotherapy, it seems to be an essential one.

In *psychoanalytic therapies*, the state is evoked when the focus is on specific details, especially memories and emotions. In other words, the focus is on one thing at a time. Questions and directions, such as "What comes?" and "Feel your feelings," will heighten it. It's the specificity that counts. Having a patient describe the details in a memory scene—colors, shapes, textures, exact locations of objects—leads, of course, to her focusing on one thing at a time and deepens the trance. When the patient is in this receptive state, often when the analyst has been silent for a long time, a comment by the analyst such as "Yes!" can have great impact.

In *cognitive therapies* the receptive state is evoked when the focus is on cognitive processes, such as inner dialogue. Either with or without some "relaxation" preamble, the patient may learn to redirect his own thought processes. As I have noted, the substitution of a good idea for a bad idea takes place most effectively when the patient is in a receptive state.

In *behavioral therapies* the receptive state is evoked in the interactions between therapist and patient as they seek and explore the value of various tasks. The focus may be on the precise method for carrying out a behavioral prescription. The linking of learned imagery-evoked comfort with images of being in the symptom-evoking situation also occurs most easily when the patient is in a receptive state.

In *solution-oriented therapies*, the trance state is evoked when the patient is directed to focus on inner processes, mostly imagery, with questions such as, "If your problems were solved magically, how would your life be different?" Even better, "When your problems or symptoms are resolved, how is your life different?"

Relaxation therapies involve a direct application of familiar trance evoking suggestions—focusing attention on one part of the body at a time for example, as in progressive relaxation. Then the use of the post-hypnotic cues, which I have called "switches" will bring back the relaxed state

Thinking

The last time I saw Erickson he explained to me the reasons for the establishment of his teaching seminars:

> I had to spend too much time on one patient. I would rather teach a lot of people how to think, how to handle problems. I have dozens and dozens of letters saying, "You have completely changed my way of treating patients." I get a lot of patients, but I see them less. I see more patients and I see them for shorter times. When I asked him, "And this is the result of …?" he answered, "Their coming here and letting me tell them stories. Then they go home and alter their practice."
>
> *(Rosen, 1982, p. 25)*

I believe that Erickson applied the same approaches to teaching therapists how to think as he did to treating patients. In both situations, the goal was to teach us how to handle problems and how to think. In order to do this, he indicated, "First you model the patient's world. Then you role model the patient's world" (Rosen, 1982, p. 35). Frequently the modeling and role-modeling were done through the medium of storytelling, through the use of teaching tales.

When Erickson told his stories, we, his audience, in the manner of American Indian children listening to an elder telling tribal tales, were enchanted, enthralled—hypnotized, in fact. He felt, and the results confirmed, that people are more open to learning when in a trance state. Thus, he would put us into a trance and provide himself as a role-model of someone who knew how to think and how to handle problems. When I once asked him what he would do when he ran into a problem that he could not solve, he role-modeled then too, answering, "I turn it over to my unconscious mind." In other words, when he could not handle a problem in his usual state of consciousness he would enter into a trance and find his answers there.

It seems that Erickson applied the same process to thinking as did my son, when, at age four, I once asked him what he wanted to do and he answered, "I'll have to ask my mind."

Obviously, just going into a trance by itself will not necessarily lead to solution of problems. When I am teaching automatic writing and direct students to simply go into a trance and write whatever comes, they frequently come up with very global statements, such as "LOVE EVERYTHING."

There are different kinds of thinking: There is the thinking that enables us to approach tasks and causes us to feel interested in or motivated toward the accomplishment of these tasks. There is the thinking that constitutes a kind of inner entertainment that is satisfying in itself, as an activity in itself. Like the thinking about thinking that I did as I was writing this article.

How then, did Erickson instruct us to think effectively and usefully? "Take a good book," he suggested, "by an author you like and respect, and read the last chapter first. Then speculate about what is in the chapter before that. Then read that chapter and speculate about what was in the chapter before that ..." (personal communication, 1977) and so on. In other words, think of your goal first. Subordinate everything else to that. When you go into trance, indicate your goal to your unconscious mind and then work backward until you reach your first steps.

"Learn from experience, not from books" (personal communication, 1977), Erickson told me. The study of philosophy may be interesting but it does not teach anyone how to think. We must discover the modes and ways of thinking that work for us—that is, that enable us to function best, to feel good about ourselves, that make us feel that we are ourselves.

In order to think about a particular issue or to think in a certain way, we need to enter into the state in which we can best do the appropriate kind of thinking. In other words, we need to access the learnings that are associated with the required state. We may enter into a general hypnotic state by utilizing one or more of the inductions that I have alluded to, and then we may focus on a switch or several switches that evoke more specific learnings.

For example, if I want to enter into an article-writing state. I may first sit at a particular desk or table that 1 have associated with this task. This alone may act as a "switch" to evoke the state. If not, I may go through some preparatory ritual—e.g., clearing the desk, having pens and paper available, perhaps in a special place. I will then enter into a trance simply by focusing attention on the paper, the pen tip, or the computer screen. I do not have to spell out for my unconscious mind the request: "I would like to come up with and record the most relevant, comprehensive material and do it in the clearest, best organized, most easily comprehended form." My unconscious mind is already aware that I want these things.

I remember the advice that Elie Wiesel once gave me about writing:

> The problem is not that you do not have enough to say but you have too much to say. And if you edit yourself you block yourself. So write out everything that comes to you, without judgment, put it aside for a while and then edit it the way you would edit the work of a stranger.

Or putting the above into the language that I have been discussing, "Go into a free-associating state, with the understanding that whatever emerges will relate to the topic you are addressing. Record what comes. Later enter into an editing state."

If I were not able to enter into the desired state, I might add some conscious suggestions or requests to my unconscious mind. For example, I might remind myself of the suggestion that Erickson gave himself when he was asked, at the last minute to speak at a college commencement: "I know how to speak." I could change this to: "I know how to write." I also could add other suggestions such as: "You have all the time that you need to think about this subject, in this case the subject of thinking itself, and to come up with some ideas that may be helpful to others also."

You will note that I am careful to avoid making too heavy demands on my unconscious, as I might have when I was younger, demands that were connected with trying to be brilliant or even to have the last word to say on this or any other subject. My life experience has taught me that this is not likely to happen and that even if it were possible it would not be desirable. At the same time, I have learned to value my unconscious mind sufficiently to know and expect that it can and will fulfill the modest request for "some useful ideas", "ideas that may be helpful to others."

Hopefully, the ideas that I have already mentioned will fulfill this request.

How about applying my model to other objects of thinking? How would we apply this model to solving a problem in treatment of a patient? We could enter into a trance by focusing on our memory of the patient's face or his way of breathing, or by focusing on our feeling of confusion or blockage. If we want to or need to go through a more formalized series of steps, we might ask our unconscious mind if it is ready and able to come up with possible solutions. If we have already worked out a way in which our unconscious is able to signal "Yes" or "No," with ideomotor signaling, for example, we would await a "Yes" response (e.g., upward movement of the right thumb). After the "Yes" response, we could notice sensations, mental images, and thoughts, assuming that they are providing the answers.

For example, with a patient who was blocked in dealing with his feeling of having been humiliated by an officer during World War II, I found myself coming up with the image of him shooting the official. I shared this with the patient and he began a new profession, that of shooting pictures of objects that are generally ignored—manhole covers, cracked walls, and so on. As he gave value to these objects, his self-esteem rose, especially as his photos were valued by others.

Steps for Thinking About What to Do Next

1. Enter into a trance by focusing on any one thing inside or out-e.g., by focusing on an issue that needs to be decided.
2. Note what comes to you. It could be some simple sensation, like the tingling sensations I noticed in my fingers once, when I experienced a writing block. It could be a story. Or it could be something as simple as a command, such as, "Do it now."

3. Ask yourself what the story or the sensations are trying to tell you. For example, the tingling sensations were present in the spots that would be touched if I were holding a pen.
4. Act on that command. Or utilize the new information. After writing a few sentences with a pen, I was able to go back to using a typewriter.

We limit ourselves so much. Erickson said, "Most of your life is unconsciously determined" (Rosen, 1982, p. 25). These unconscious self-limitations prevent us from "thinking big," for example. Yet there are some people who think big automatically. "Think and grow rich." It does not take only thinking big. One must so develop one's abilities and skills and be willing and able to make the effort required. But, if one does not dare to think about thinking big, even with effort, one will stop short of really "growing rich." One will be frightened by the prospect of success and will subsequently stop short, often far short, of achieving it.

One way of going beyond learned limitations is to play, to make-believe, to tell ourselves that whatever we do or say is not serious and that we won't be held to account for it. This, by the way, is generally a good way to think creatively. And why should we not think creatively all the time? We won't wear out our ability to think. In fact, we will sharpen it.

You may well ask, "How do I go about doing this?" Or, as a therapist, "How can I help my patients do this?"

One way is to go back to the beginnings of your learning. Apply the principle that is mentioned in the Early Learning Set Induction. "Many of the things that you now do automatically once required conscious mental effort." Therefore, to change a pattern of indecisiveness, go into a light trance when you need to make a decision—e.g., ordering in a restaurant, or deciding what movie you want to see. You can do this simply by focusing attention on the question itself: "What would I like to order?" This constitutes focusing attention on one thing. You may have to do this a dozen times, on a dozen different occasions, before the process becomes automatic, but when you discover that it is, you will experience a wonderful feeling of delight. The conscious mental effort of putting yourself into a trance and querying your unconscious mind will have been well rewarded.

In general, Erickson gave us many guides that can help us to think more flexibly, with more openness. We can stretch our minds by solving puzzles, by thinking of as many ways as is possible of accomplishing different tasks by using certain words. For example, one can think about how many different ways we could use the word "No," or how many ways we could go from one room to another. Or we can try to solve one of Erickson's favorite puzzles: How would you plant 10 trees in 5 rows, 4 in a row. (Answer: a 5-pointed star.)

We can look at things from different perspectives. Betty Erickson gave me an old book that Erickson liked to give out. It is titled *Topsys and Turvys* and is made up of pictures, with subtexts. When turned upside down, the pictures change and the subtexts complete a two-line poem. For example, one caption reads, "The

Malay pirate eyed his foes in hopeless fierce despair." When turned upside down, the picture is different and is described by a caption reading, "Till—bang!—his magazine blew up, and hurled the crew in air" (Newell, 1964).

Looking at optical illusions can help us to loosen up our mental processes. Practicing the exercises in books such as Reid J. Daitzman's *Mental Jogging* (New York: Marek, 1980) may be helpful.

All the exercises and approaches I have mentioned are best done, I have found, when you enter into a trance. As usual the trance can be attained by focusing attention on one thing, which could be some aspect of the puzzle, or on the illusion itself.

So, read good books. Listen to good music. Associate with good people. I say the above with the realization that each of us will have his or her idea of what is good. The principle that I am emphasizing is: "Positive input is important."

We don't really know much about thinking, just as we don't know much about hypnosis. Forty years ago, I concluded that if I could understand hypnosis, I would be able to understand thinking. Since then I—and you—have learned something about both. I suppose that hypnosis can be thought of as some form or way of thinking. We have learned more about the neurological underpinnings of thinking. For example, we know something about left and right brain functioning. We are learning about neurotransmitters and neural plasticity, but, I'm afraid that still today, I feel the same way. I'm still hoping that some real understanding will be attained in my lifetime. Meanwhile, I'm enjoying applying the bit of understanding I have achieved for the enrichment of my life and that of others.

Note

1 This chapter was previously published in *Ericksonian Methods: The Essence of the Story*, edited by Jeffrey Zeig, as Chapter 22, pp. 333–348.

References

Beahrs, J.O., and Humiston, K.E. (1972). Dynamics of experiential therapy. *American Journal of Clinical Hypnosis*, 17(1): 1–14.

Damon, S.F. (1971). *A Blake Dictionary: The Ideas and Symbols of William Blake*. New York: Dutton.

Erickson, M.H., and Rossi, E.L. (1979). *Hypnotherapy: An Exploratory Casebook*. New York: Irvington.

Hilgard, E.R. (1968). *The Experience of Hypnosis*. New York: Harcourt Brace Jovanovich.

Keynes, G. (ed.) (1969). *Complete Writings of William Blake, with variant readings*. Oxford: Oxford University Press.

Newell, P. (1964). *Topsys and Turvys*. New York: Dover.

Orne, M. (1962). On the Social Psychology of the Psychological Experiment: With Particular Reference to Demand Characteristics and their Implications. *American Psychologist*, 17(11): 776–783.

Rosen, S. (1982) *My Voice Will Go with You: The Teaching Tales of Milton H. Erickson*. New York: Norton.

4

CONCRETIZING OF SYMPTOMS AND THEIR MANIPULATION[1]

Introduction

Why is it helpful to symbolize and concretize a symptom? When we symbolize and concretize a symptom we can do something with it, such as change it or manipulate it.

This chapter begins with the example of Sara, an ex-nun who dealt with her negative experiences by having them symbolized as clothing, and then concretized as a pile of underwear. She concretized the symbol by changing from seeing a pile of clothing to feeling or even smelling it, which appeared to her as concrete. At that point, with the help of another patient, also an ex-nun, Erickson helped Sara remove some of her clothing from the pile, which I call the manipulation of the concretized symbol. In this way, she was able to diminish her negative experiences. It wasn't until Sara saw the clothing as a concrete article—underwear—that she could manipulate it and remove it from the pile. Once it was concrete, she could change the way she visualized and experienced it, taking out of the realm of being a thought process to a process that was more manageable.

Other patients, too, are able to manipulate their symbols after concretizing them, such as the patient who had abdominal pain which she was able to concretize as a red color in a pen. We could then have a "scribble" until all the red was gone.

Pain is concretized as a red pen, hair pulling is concretized as a bird, and the fear of heights of another patient is concretized by seeing a connection between a fear-inducing ladder and a relaxing canoe. Many of the treatments described in this chapter involve concretizing a symptom and then leaving it behind. Once it has been concretized, a symbol is open for manipulation such as being left behind or changing a painful color to a peaceful one. These examples are illustrations of the power of imagination, which William Blake and others have emphasized. Jacob Bronowski, who wrote extensively about Blake, states in *The Origins of Knowledge and Imagination* that visual imagination is the most powerful human faculty, which no other animal shares with us. "We cannot separate the special importance of the visual apparatus of man from his unique ability to imagine, to make plans, and to do all the other things which are generally included in the catchall phrase 'free will'," Bronowski writes. "What we really mean by free will, of course, is the visualizing of alternatives and making a choice between them. In my view, which not everyone shares, the central problem of human consciousness depends on this ability to imagine" (Bronowski 1979, p. 18).

The ability to manipulate concretized symbols shows that thoughts can indeed affect reality. On one level, as classically liberal political thinkers such as John Stuart Mill have emphasized, you are not responsible for what you think, only for what you do. But, as Erickson recognized, what you think can become part of your experience so it's felt as a reality that you are actually living. What you think becomes part of your experience, especially if you concretize it. In this positive sense, you can take responsibility for what you think. Particularly when what you think is experienced as a concrete or symbolic object, you can be responsive to what you think.

We are not responsible for our initial thoughts, which may come from bodily sensations, from the unconscious, or from dreams that we don't consciously create. But we can take responsibility for concretizing a thought after it presents itself, and then altering it. Erickson's insight was that you need to concretize a thought before you can change it. You can't just say you want to think differently.

It's liberating to discover that we have the opportunity to alter our thoughts and our emotions by concretizing them. Although we're not responsible for causing our involuntary thoughts, we can change them into concrete images to which we can respond and which we have the power to alter in positive ways.

∗∗∗

I was first impressed with the possibility of treating symptoms as concrete realities after reading about Erickson's 1966 treatment (Erickson, 1980a) of a woman who was bedeviled with hallucinations of naked men who flew around after her. Erickson told her that she could leave her naked men in his closet and return regularly to ensure that they were still there. As a result, she was free of hallucinations and was able to work and conduct a relatively normal life. When she moved to another state, he had her mail her hallucinations to him and he kept the envelopes, knowing that she would, come back some day to see them. His contact with her continued for more than 25 years. Because Erickson had treated the hallucinations as real objects, they could be locked in a closet and shipped in an envelope. They could, in other words, be manipulated. I have applied this same principle with many patients who were not psychotic but who were suffering from extreme anxiety, pain, or depression. I have found it especially effective with patients who, in deep trance states, get in touch with material which their conscious mind is not yet able to tolerate and which consequently causes them significant discomfort. These are patients who would call between sessions complaining that they felt "unreal" or fearing that they might lose their minds. Suggestions of amnesia for the disturbing material often are helpful, but in some cases, these are not enough. In a trance state I suggest to them that they leave their symptom or the material that is emerging *here* in my office. I tell them that we will work on their deep troubling problems here, in my office. During the week, between sessions, they are to live their life, as comfortably as possible, "not needing to think about these things."

The process of concretizing and manipulating symptoms stems partly from Erickson's observation that hypnotized subjects often respond literally. (Erickson, 1980b) A more recent study by McCue and McCue found that this tendency toward literalism may be dependent on the way that suggestions are presented. (McCue, 1988) Thus, Erickson's subjects may have responded literally because he expected them to do so. (We know that hypnotized subjects are often eager to do what they sense the hypnotist expects.) In any case, hypnotized subjects do show the capacity, whether due to trance characteristics or demand characteristics, to think and respond "concretely," in a way characteristic of some schizophrenics and many brain-damaged patients. For example, when a hypnotized subject is asked, "What do you feel?" he or she may respond with, "the wool of my trousers." In these situations, literalness and concreteness seem to be practically synonymous.

It is, of course, possible to give suggestions in ways to ensure that they are likely to be taken literally and so that images are concretized. We may start by suggesting to the patient that he simply "imagine" a color or form that is connected with a symptom or quality of a symptom. Then we may gradually lead the patient to the perception that the form is the symptom or the quality, or that the quality (strength, anxiety, etc.) is embedded in that form. The concretizing is encouraged by having the patient focus on details, perhaps even specifying each of the senses—sight, hearing, smell, and touch.

Whether or not concretizing is an automatic aspect of imaging in hypnosis or whether it is simply easier to concretize in a trance, this tendency can be utilized in treatment. After we have concretized the symptom, we can change its size, shape, color, location, function, motility, and so on. In short, we can manipulate it. For example, a patient with a headache could be directed to see it, concretely, as a red ball and might then image the ball as rolling down a hill, far away from his or her aching head. We could suggest that the pain, embedded in the ball, could be disposed of in this way. Remarkably, the patient often will be relieved of the headache.

Physical Objects That Embody Concretized Qualities and Forces

As with other phenomena that we observe with hypnosis, the tendency to concretize occurs naturally in many other areas of human activity, especially in the promotion of healing and the search for wisdom and security. For example, individuals throughout the ages have sought security and magical protection by touching objects such as touchstones, rabbits' feet, and wood. For some people these objects actually embody the comfort, safety, protection, or good luck they seek. The animal symbols in Shinto religion, the symbols of Kaballa in Judaism, and the symbols used by "witch doctors" and shamans also can be seen as examples of concretizing. They offer a wide range of modalities for tapping into the unconscious and for accessing and changing symptoms and resources. Stevens and Stevens have noted how shamans operate on the belief that:

> all elements have their source in the spirit world and therefore are infused with spirits that can be contacted for any number of purposes.
> [...]
> [E]ach form [of air] may be called upon for its unique contribution of knowledge. Light breezes, whirlwinds, and cold winds.... Each form has a special store of wisdom that may be garnered by forming a relationship with it. By acknowledging the wind and talking to it, shamans gain in wisdom, power, and mastery because they know what the wind knows.
> *(Stevens and Stevens, 1988, p. 82)*

In concretizing symptoms, it is useful to remember that some individuals may prefer to use mental imagery while others may prefer actual physical representations. Perhaps there is a parallel with the use of religious objects, including paintings and sculptures of deities. Many years ago, in Kyoto, I talked with a leader of the Shin Buddhist group, which, I believe, is the largest Buddhist group, in Japan. I commented on my observation that Shin, like Catholicism in the West, seemed to utilize statues and religious objects more than other religions. His response was, "Some people can feel closeness and love by simply thinking of their beloved. Others feel it better by looking at a picture." Perhaps the religions that utilize real external objects of worship have the largest numbers of followers because they offer the opportunity for both ways of relating to the deity or worshipped one—both through abstractions and through concretizing.

Symbolizing and Concretizing

Is concretizing the same as symbolizing? I believe that they are both part of the same process and that the difference between them may be mainly one of degree. A country, for example, can be symbolized in the form of a flag. Thereafter, the display of that flag may evoke patriotic feelings whereas desecration of the flag-symbol may evoke rage. But if a flag desecrator or a patriot were to believe that destruction of a flag was the same as actually damaging the country or threatening its existence, he or she would be concretizing that symbol. Similarly, an emotion can be symbolized by being put into words. But then the word "joy" is not, itself, joy. It does not even contain a substance that could be experienced as "joy." The map is not the territory (Korsybski, 1933). However, if a person can experience the word itself as containing the quality of joy, then that emotion has been concretized—in the form of that word.

Once I had a patient who tended to concretize even without a hypnotic induction. She felt devastated when she was rejected by a man in whom she was interested. I asked her to close her eyes and tell me what she saw and how she felt. She saw the word "LOVE," broken in two, with the letters "VE" having separated from the "LO" and fallen down. She felt sad, heavy, hopeless. I suggested that she repair the word—raise the "VE" and stick the letters to the beginning of the word. She did this and reported that she felt content, happy, and light. Thus, the concretizing process by which the patient represented loss was used to effect positive changes.

In a related application I once witnessed Erickson therapeutically move a student/patient from symbolizing to concretizing (Rossi, 1978). The patient, an ex-nun ("Sara"), was first hypnotically reoriented to a road beside a river she had previously described in detail. Erickson then suggested that Sara

> walk about 50 yards down the wash and look back to see what you've left behind you. When Sara saw some shoes, Erickson had her play with that image for a while, asking her if the shoes were moving. At first she said that they were not, then she said, laughingly, that they were dancing. After making certain that she could clearly visualize this, he again repeated his suggestion, but in a different form: "Now walk down the wash about 70 feet, and you will have left behind you something very important to you … and look back and tell me what you've left behind you."

At first Sara responded that she thought she had left her fear behind. She said, "The thing that comes to my mind is my fear and what I see is outer clothing. I guess it's like that's symbolic. And my wish is that that would be so." So far, she was symbolizing, not concretizing.

She went on, observing, "I see a pile." When asked to elaborate, she described the contents of the clothing pile, which included some underwear. As she described these intimate details, we observers got the definite feeling that she could see, feel, and perhaps even smell the clothing. The clothing appeared concrete, real. At this point she had moved toward what I call "concretizing."

Erickson then evoked the help of Dora, another ex-nun who was present, to help Sara remove some of her clothing from the pile. This action is what I refer to as the "manipulation of the concretized symbol."

Similar strategies can be used with patients suffering from symptom complexes such as depression, phobias, pain, and anxiety. Such patients often describe concrete aspects of their suffering. For example, a depressed person will feel a heavy weight on his or her back or chains around his or her chest. A patient with extreme anxiety may feel "tied up in knots" or a knotting in the abdomen. The therapist does not need to work toward the creation of new concrete images, but can simply have the patient see or feel the chains being cast off or the knots being untied, cut, or displaced to the outside.

When the concretizing of symptoms does not occur spontaneously, the therapist can help to develop some concrete forms in which to embody them. This can be done most directly by having the patient focus on the symptom. For example, the therapist might suggest the following: "As you are concentrating on your pain, can you note the shape of it? Does it have a color? Does it move, or is it still? Hot or cold? What image comes to you as you are doing this?"

Patients sometimes come up with surprising, idiosyncratic images: dancing bananas, weeping rocks, and so on. Depression may be concretized as smoke or as a weight; anxiety may be concretized as flashing colored lights, or electricity, or as a buzzing noise.

Symptoms also can be concretized in the form of written descriptions, in imagination or in actuality. The descriptions then can be disposed of by being launched in a rocket or balloon, buried or burned. Or they can be revised. The sentence "I am helpless," for example, can be changed to "I am competent." Simple as this sounds, this mental manipulation of word symbols while in a trance often can be effective.

Another strategy is to find colors that represent the symptoms. The colors, which may or may not be connected with an object, can be altered. The red of pain or anxiety may be faded as one looks at a field of red tulips, so that in the distance the tulips appear pink and finally white. It is remarkable how often this simple approach will lead to immediate relief of a headache or the ending of a panic attack.

Concretizing of Resources

Just as a phobic situation or word may trigger panic, a positive association, connected with a concrete object, may trigger healthy, comforting responses. Everyday examples include the practice of touching something, as in the already mentioned superstition of knocking wood. In some cases, this will evoke a feeling of reassurance (or "real-assurance," the assurance that one is real). In fact, touching some concrete or "real" object can be especially helpful with patients who are disturbed by panic-evoking feelings of unreality. These patients can, for example, literally and figuratively "get in touch" with themselves by touching one hand against the other. In other words, one's own body can be felt and utilized as a concrete resource.

Natural omnipresent elements such as air and water are especially useful as concretizing resources. Air can be experienced as peace or calm inducing and may be especially helpful in dealing with anxiety, with a smoking habit, or with any condition that involves taking something into the body. In the form of wind or simply in its stillness, air can be experienced as a vehicle for inspiration (literally "breathing in"). Similarly, drinking or sipping water can give a person a sense of relaxation or fulfillment. With appropriate imagery and association practice, even a feeling of intoxication can be achieved by drinking water.

One of the best ways to find resources that may replace or alleviate a symptom is to have patients search for "unconscious learnings" by going back to a time when they have felt secure, comfortable, and warm inside. They can find images that come to them as they do this. I call the images that trigger the desired effect "positive triggers" or "positive switches"; they are forms of posthypnotic cues. Often these "switches" can be concretized. For example, the sensation of holding a rag doll from childhood may be recalled and then transferred to a ball of wool or some other object that the patient can carry or touch.

Concretizing of Resources in Cancer Patients

Immune stimulating forces or healing forces may be visualized or thought of as little animals or fish, such as "blue sharks" (Achterberg, 1985; Simonton, Simonton, & Creighton, 1978). Technological powers such as those connected with laser beams are often visualized. The cancer itself can be seen as wild animals, which can then be tamed, eaten by the sharks, or diminished in size by laser beams. In the form of a monster, the cancer may be transformed by some technical or magical means into a smaller, weaker form of the same animal or into another harmless or even a helping animal—a nursing mother lion, for example. The patient might imaginably "become" a lion cub who is strengthened by the milk he receives from the nursing mother. Along the same lines the injected chemotherapy fluids can be experienced as that nourishing and strengthening milk.

Case Examples

To illustrate how these concretizing techniques can be used, some case examples may be helpful.

A Patient with Abdominal Pain

THERAPIST: Find a color that comes to your mind while you're focusing on that pain ... Red? Think of an object or some objects that are colored red. What comes to you now?
PATIENT: A pen.
T: A red pen? Does it write in red ink also?
P: Yes.
T: Pick up the pen and write, in red ink, some words, such as "comfort," "peace," or you may just want to scribble or make some wavy lines until all

54 Concretizing of Symptoms and Their Manipulation

the red is gone from that pen. As the red leaves the pen it can be interesting to wonder, "Will my pain leave my abdomen also?"

When the pain is very much less in your abdomen, then your right thumb can go up as a signal. (Thumb goes up.)

When you're ready, you can come out of your trance and leave that pen and that pain behind you and you can look forward to dealing with black ink and being in the black. Put some of the situations you've been dealing with into a black hole. And you can know that it's alright for you to succeed. It's alright for you to be happy. It's not written anywhere that you cannot succeed, and if it is written anywhere that can be erased, can't it? And you can replace it with black ink.

(After the patient comes out of trance)

T: How does your abdomen feel now?
P: It's fine. It doesn't hurt.
T: And that took only about 10 minutes.
P: It felt real bad before.

A Hair-Pulling Compulsion (Trichotillomania)

The patient, a 38-year-old professional woman, sought help in overcoming a hair-pulling compulsion. She also is a compulsive worker and suffers from several psychosomatic ailments, including allergic skin reactions, asthma, and obesity. In previous hypnotic work the patient and I had agreed that her thumbs could move, automatically, to signal "yes" via the right thumb and "no" with the left thumb.

T: You can take that hair-pulling compulsion and put it into some form, if you like. It could be a form which would apply to and which could represent the hair-pulling compulsion. When you have found such a form, you can let your right thumb go up, as a signal. (Pause—20 seconds. Right thumb moves up.) Tell me about it, if you like.
P: Interesting—it's a bird.
T: Does it have a color?
P: Red.
T: Like a cardinal? A scarlet tanager? A red bird.
P: Mmm.
T: Well, we certainly do not want to put a wild bird into a cage. What can we do with that bird ... to let it keep its energy ... and freedom, while letting go of its destructive elements.
P: We could feed it and take care of it.
T: That does not mean feeding your body, does it? Substituting overeating for pulling. How could you feed that bird without hurting yourself?
P: Give it gradually increasing increments of food.

T: Small increments of nutrients.
P: Enough space to explore and exercise.
T: Uh-hun. Can you come up with some ritual or movement or an image which could provide the small increments of nutrients and enough space to explore? How would you represent that?
P: Just picturing the bird.
T: When you see that bird, does the impulse to play with your hair become more or less?
P: Less.
T: Would visualizing the bird be enough to take away or stop your impulse?
P: (no answer)
T: Just thinking about it. Would that help?
P: I see it pecking at me. Fluttering around.
T: Pecking at your hair?
P: Yes.
T: So I'd suggest that you picture that bird, pecking at your hair ... and fluttering around ... and see to what extent that diminishes your impulse to touch your hair. It may get rid of it entirely. You could redirect your hair pulling energy toward that image. Will you do that?
P: Yes.
T: Can you see yourself and experience yourself doing it right now?
P: (right thumb up)
T: And is the impulse toward your hair ... is it diminished or gone?
P: Gone.
T: Gone. Good. And every time you do this it's very likely that the same thing will happen as is happening right now. You can get that same feeling of pleasure ... watching that bird pecking.... So that you don't have to peck at yourself.... And you can vicariously enjoy the sense of freedom that the bird has also ... can't you? And all it needs is small increments of nutrition. In fact, if you start to identify with the bird, I wonder if it might not be helpful for you to start to eat like a bird. And enjoy that. Because you'll then get the extra pleasure of seeing and feeling your weight diminish.... And the sense of lightness and freedom could reflect in your breathing more easily also. Feeling lighter. More open. It will be very interesting to explore that, won't it? And all this can revolve around the image which you've created, which you've just created, just come up with yourself. It is your image ... it is your bird. It's your opportunity to utilize it for your benefit. (Each time I asked "isn't it?" or "won't it?" the patient's right thumb went up.)

Interestingly, during the next four months the patient not only stopped her hair pulling, but also lost about 20 pounds. She found that she was no longer interested in nibbling food, and she ate sparingly, but enjoyably, at

56 Concretizing of Symptoms and Their Manipulation

regular meals. Her breathing difficulties were considerably relieved and she required less medication.

Fear of Height and Allergic Reactions

The patient was an artist suffering from various allergies (skin and upper respiratory) as well as from a fear of heights which was severe enough to interfere with her being able to work on a ladder.

T: When you are in at least a moderately deep trance your right thumb can go up as a signal. That's right ... deeper ... and deeper ... and deeper ... good. And are you now in a sufficiently deep trance now, so that your unconscious mind can, and is able to, relieve your allergic symptoms to a great degree?
P: (right thumb goes up)
T: Good. So I don't have to tell your unconscious how to do that, do I? It knows how, doesn't it? You may want to help it a little bit by focusing on some images, breathing sea air, while standing on a beach, breathing in air that is not permeated with allergens of any kind ... clean fresh air, healthy air. As you do that your nose opens up. Your head begins to clear. It feels good, doesn't it? A cool breeze blowing across your forehead. You can have a warm feeling inside your abdomen.... Breathing becomes easier and easier, so that you feel really relaxed, calm and comfortable ... and as you feel more relaxed and calm, your head becomes even more clear. Breathing becomes still more open. *You can take those allergic symptoms and put them into some form or other.* You can see something or can conceive of some form that represents your allergy symptoms. When you can do that, let your right thumb go up. Color ... form ... beginning to form itself. More and more clearly ... (long pause) ... that's right. And while you're doing that, you can put into that same form your fear of heights, if you like. Add it on or stick it in there. You can evoke that fear by picturing yourself on a very high point ... right.... What image comes with that?
   Can you attach that to the other form? The one that represents the allergies? (Right thumb goes up) Good. You can see it, can't you?
P: I see a big red circle.
T: A big red circle. Is it shaded, or is it evenly red?
P: It looks hot and there's yellow in the center.
T: Alright. A big red circle. Hot and yellow ... alright now ... can you conceive of a symbol, or another image that represents security ... and freedom ... and openness. The ability to breathe freely?
P: (right thumb up)
T: That's right. What do you see now? Is it your "power piece"? (a piece of jewelry)
P: A canoe.

Concretizing of Symptoms and Their Manipulation 57

T: A canoe. (pause) So all you have to do is transform that circle into a canoe.... When you've done that, let your right thumb go up.... It's not easy, but you can do it (pause) That's right.... (thumb goes up) Yes. Good. And every time you touch that power piece it could remind you of a canoe. It has a similar shape, doesn't it? So, you have at least two ways of evoking your canoe. You can do it just mentally ... or with the help of a touch ... and as you come out of your trance, by counting from 20 to 1, you can bring back that knowledge with you, that readiness ... to feel secure, to breathe easily ... to be reminded of that, by calling upon your canoe. You'll do that, won't you?

P: (right thumb goes up)

T: Good. So I will count from 20 to 1. You can let your eyes open on the count of 1 feeling relaxed, alert, refreshed, and wider and wider awake. 20, 19, 18, 17, 16 (then faster) 15, 14, 13, 12, 11,10,9,8,7,6, 5, 4, 3, 2, 1. And, while you are feeling strong and secure and well supported, you might, after a moment, picture yourself on the top of that ladder, working on your painting. Focusing on the painting. Not needing to think about it. Realizing that you are secure.

P: I saw a connection between the ladder and the canoe also.

T: Yes?

P: It was sort of funny. It's uh ... totally irrational. Completely irrational. But you'll understand it. What I was seeing was a canoe ... that was ... I couldn't get it to be a red canoe, and I have seen red canoes. The old ones, the heavier ones were painted. They were wood, but they were painted. Red or green usually.

T: Green, yeah.

P: But, by the time I was in camp, we also had aluminum canoes. Which was why it was so funny, because they were lighter to pick up and were easier to deal with.

T: Right.

P: In my mind, all the time I thought, "How can I get that circle to turn into a canoe?" which I eventually was able to make a red canoe out of it. But I kept seeing the ladder. And I have a wonderful wooden ladder. That's the very big one. It's the wooden one. The one that I usually use, that doesn't frighten me, but I don't go up that high, is aluminum, but it's not as big as the one I'm using now.

T: Mmhmm.

P: I thought for a minute, "How funny, because the ladder looks more like a canoe."

T: Because it's made of wood.

P: Yeah, but that's the thing that's so irrational. This looks like, it looks like wood. Yeah. It's a church ladder. A library ladder. It's a great big oak—huge. It's a big thing that stands. And it has a flat top. Very, very big.

T: Maybe it looks like a canoe if you put it on its side?

P: Well it could look more like a canoe, because it looks really like.... Oh, God! ... (whispered) I totally forgot! It's like in your picture! (a painting on my wall which she had done.) Oh, I can't believe it! It's so funny!

T: It's alright You can take the picture with you, in your mind ... and let me know how comfortable you really feel the next time you get up there on that ladder.

As can be seen in the transcript, the patient and I found several concrete representations of security, in her mental imagery and also in my office, which itself represented and evoked a feeling of security. The fact that we were finally able to bring together an actual creation of her own—the canoe in her/my painting—undoubtedly added to the power of this concretized representation of security. In any case, she reported at the next session that she had lost her fear of working on the tall ladder and her allergic condition had gone into a stage of remission.

A Cancer Patient with Nausea as the Result of Chemotherapy

(The nausea was intensified after her boss's wife had attacked her verbally, questioning her intelligence, competence, and sincerity.)

T: And now you might focus on that nausea, you can feel it in your throat, in the pit of your stomach, your chest, perhaps.... And, as you focus on it, you notice that it tends to increase, doesn't it? But, as you are focusing on it, you can see an object or symbol or color ... some kind of object, perhaps, that represents the nausea When you see that, tell me what it is ... put the nausea into some form or other.

P: I just see a pyramid.

T: What color is the pyramid?

P: Gold.

T: Alright. Pyramid shaped and gold in color. Is the surface rough or smooth?

P: Rough.

T: Does the pyramid seem to be made out of real gold, or is it just gold in color?

P: Color.

T: It's a little bit like a yellow color, isn't it? Like the color of vomit? (patient nods) Now, what I think I'd like to ask your unconscious mind to do is to change the color of that pyramid ... perhaps to a color like blue ... or any other color than gold. When you can see that new color let your right thumb go up....

P: (thumb up)

T: Good. What color do you see?

P: Red.

T: Red.... And then ... let the red become diluted ... until it becomes a pink, perhaps a skin color eventually.... Or it may even disappear altogether ...

Concretizing of Symptoms and Their Manipulation 59

fade away and be replaced by air, or sky blue. Just notice the changes as they occur. (pause) What color do you see now?

P: No color.

T: Good. So that now you can see ...

P: (clears throat)

T: It's alright to clear your throat. Breathe in that clear air, that clear atmosphere. It could have a calming effect, as it goes into your throat, down into your stomach; it may warm your stomach on the inside ... soothe your stomach. You can become more and more comfortable, with every breath that you take in ... clean, healing air ... and when that nausea is gone completely ...

P: (swallows and looks restless)

T: Not yet. Is it getting worse again?

P: (left thumb goes up to indicate "No")

T: What's happening now? (tears are seen in patient's eyes) The nausea is being replaced by some emotion?

P: I just feel teary.

T: And the tears can keep on flowing, like the waters of the Nile. You started with pyramids. But, as you picture that river, flowing, constantly flowing, you know that it will go on ... and on and on, until eventually it leads to an ocean. You might even want to go for a swim in that ocean, as I did when I was in Elat, in Israel, years ago. You can imagine yourself, in any case, being cooled and rested as you swim, or float, or just bathe in the fresh, clear, healing water.

P: It seems that someone is always shooting at you.

T: When you're between the Israelis and the Arabs, that's what happens.... There are people who are going to be shooting at you, that's true. When you are surrounded by vicious, nasty people. Self-centered people. But you don't have to just stay out there as a target. You may decide to just duck under the water for a while. You could enter into a submarine and go under cover for a while. And wait until the attack blows over. That's the way her husband deals with it, isn't it He lets her spout off and ignores it. Then, an hour later, she may just be angry at something else, or somebody else, maybe. She will have forgotten about it. I don't think it's necessary to make every attack into a battle, or a war. (The patient confirmed that this is what had happened that day.)

T: Next time you are exposed to this kind of shooting it would be good to have some kind of shield.

P: A real one.

T: A real one, or at least a mental one. You could imagine yourself inside a transparent, protective, bullet-proof sphere. Just imagine yourself on the inside. She's on the outside—throwing things. Shooting. Yelling. You can't even hear her. It's soundproof also. Or, you hear her voice coming and you change it into the sound of animals. Don't listen to the words ... (two-minute pause) How does your stomach feel now? Still feel a little nauseous? That will diminish more and more. You might go back and repeat that pyramid exercise, several times a day. Visualize the pyramid. Change the color. Relax.

The patient was subsequently able to negotiate a better, less stressful job, where she did not have much contact with the boss's wife. She utilized the pyramid image before and sometimes after chemotherapy sessions and was able to complete the series of treatments with minimal side effects.

Conclusions

The process of concretizing symptoms is an effective technique, but, of course, rarely will it constitute an entire therapy. As therapists we must be familiar with many different approaches and must be judicious in deciding which ones to apply in a given case. I have given only a few examples in which concretizing of symptoms and resources has apparently expedited therapy. Obviously, even in these examples there were many other factors that contributed to the success of the therapy and even to the cooperation between patient and therapist in devising the concretizing.

It occurs to me that Erickson frequently tended to think and to express his communications to patients in literal and concrete forms. Whether or not he was correct in believing that people in trance usually responded literally, he may have been correct in assuming that the unconscious mind operates in a literal, concrete mode and that by speaking concretely we can speak more directly with the unconscious mind. Or it may be that literal and concrete formulations are effective and potent simply because they are simple and clear, or because they are similar to the way we would talk to a receptive child. I truly believe that we often can be most helpful to our patients when we talk to them as if they were children—or at least when we talk to "the child within." Perhaps this is because, as children, we were most flexible, most open and available for new learnings. The magical world of the child is approached agreeably and often elegantly with this game we play, which we call hypnosis.

Note

1 This chapter was previously published in *Brief Therapy Myths, Methods and Metaphors*, 1990, edited by Jeffrey Zeig and Stephen Gilligan as Chapter 20, pp. 258–272.

References

Achterberg, J. (1985). *Imagery in Healing: Shamanism and Modem Medicine*. Boston: New Science Library.
Bronowski, J. (1979). *The Origins of Knowledge and Imagination*. Cambridge, MA: Yale University Press.
Erickson, M. (1980a). Hypnosis: It's Renascence as a Treatment Modality. In E. Rossi (ed.), *The Collected Papers of Milton H. Erickson, Vol. 4*, pp. 70–74. New York: Irvington.

Erickson, M. (1980b). Literalness an Experimental Study. in E. Rossi (ed.), *The Collected Papers of Milton H. Erickson, Vol 3*, pp. 92–99. New York: Irvington.

Korsybski, A. (1933). *Science and Sanity*, 4th edn. Lakeville, CT: International Non Aristotelian Library Publishing Co.

McCue, P.A., and McCue, E. C. (1988). Literalness: An unsuggested (spontaneous) item of hypnotic behavior? *International Journal of Clinical and Experimental Hypnosis*, 36(3): 192–197.

Rossi, E.L. (1978). Videotape of a teaching seminar with Milton H. Erickson. Phoenix, AZ.

Simonton, O.C., Simonton, S., and Creighton, J.L. (1978). *Getting Well Again*. Los Angeles: Tarcher.

Stevens, J., and Stevens, L.S. (1988). *Secrets of Shamanism*. New York: Avon.

5

THE PSYCHOTHERAPEUTIC AND HYPNOTHERAPEUTIC APPROACHES OF MILTON H. ERICKSON, M.D.[1]

Introduction

When I was growing up in Ontario, I wasn't very good at baseball so I practiced doing magic tricks. In the process of doing magic, I found some simple pamphlets that explained how to do hypnosis. The pamphlets told you to stare at a small point of light, and they gave suggestions such as: "You are getting very tired, you feel your eyelids want to close, they close of their own weight."

When I was in pre-meds, around the age of 16, I had two friends, Jack and Art. They were unsocial enough that they also followed my interest in hypnosis. Eventually both of them went into atomic science. Art was very skeptical about hypnosis. He thought it was just putting on an act. So, I hypnotized Jack in the presence of this skeptic and I was amazed that as I talked to Jack, Art's eyes started to flutter and he seemed to be sitting there asleep with his eyes closed. He followed all the suggestions that I gave to Jack, including post hypnotic suggestions such as: After you open your eyes, I will snap my fingers and you will jump up in the air and yell "Geronimo." After Art had done precisely what I suggested, I asked him, "Why did you jump in the air?" He responded as many people do, by saying, "I was just pretending." From this I learned that conscious rejection was very often accompanied by absence of resistance.

Jack, Art and I went to the *Encyclopedia Britannica's* discussion of hypnosis. It mentioned that Erickson was a leader of hypnosis who had developed hypnotic techniques in the 1930s. Based on our talking together about hypnosis and Erickson, we all decided to see him. In the end, my mother wouldn't give me permission to travel to the United States—she worried that I could be drafted or taken into the Army, since the Second World War had begun. This would have been around 1941. But Jack and Art went to see Erickson, who spent time with both of them. He was very good that way with people. He worked the same way he did with his own children: being present, doing some kinds of experiments by himself, and testing the effects of the suggestions. Before he hypnotized my friends, he was experimenting with a lot of nonverbal suggestions, such as "you'll get up and move the lamp two feet to the right," or "you'll pull down the window shade, again." They would do all that. Afterward, Erickson explained how he had given them nonverbal suggestions to do these things. In the course of a conversation with these boys, he was always experimenting.

The word hypnosis comes from the Greek word for sleep—hypnos—and the word hypnotism was popularized in 1841 by the Scottish physician, James Braid, who followed Mesmer's techniques of animal magnetism. In India in the 1840s, British doctors did surgeries and amputations without any anesthesia except for hypnosis. Their patients seemed to be asleep and they would permit surgery to be done without screaming. Erickson, however, did not put people to sleep. He believed patients could receive suggestions as long as the unconscious mind was listening, whether or not they were asleep or even in a deep trance.

The first time I met Erickson was in 1970. I was at the Rusk Institute for Rehabilitation Medicine in New York, and I was teaching a course on hypnosis in the psychology department. When I met Erickson, he took a rubber bulb out of a desk drawer, squeezed it, and it went beep, beep.

"Every child likes a surprise," he said. He was always a prankster.

I saw him with a group of people around 1972. I was sitting in a chair next to him and he asked what I would like. I said I would like him to help me in remembering names, since I can't seem to remember names of people when I first meet them. In response to my request, he said:

> In my way of living, I like to climb a mountain. I always wonder what's on the other side. I know that on my side of the mountain, there are trees, there are grasses there are rivers, lakes, buildings, houses. On the other side of the mountain it could be a desert, dark and foreboding, and I always know that no matter how dark and foreboding the desert may be, I will find something there of value for me.

I took that to mean that there are things we know, but we don't know we know, that are in our unconscious mind. If we can tap into those learnings through hypnosis, they can be of value.

During one of our early sessions, Erickson told me the dry beds story that I recount below, about how he helped a girl stop wetting her bed. In the story, he uses imagery and imagination to embed his suggestions. He asks the young girl, who is wetting her bed, to imagine a strange man poking his head through the door, a surprise which would lead her to stop wetting her bed. Then he says you don't need a strange man poking his head in the door to stop wetting your bed. Now you know what you already knew and didn't know that you already knew it. Namely that you can stop urinating in response to any stimulus you choose. You don't need a strange man to be the stimulus: the idea of a stimulus is enough, and if you imagine it, you'll freeze.

When I tell this story to help patients overcome writers block, for example, I've left it so they can find their own stimulus or, as I call it, their own "switch," to switch off negative symptoms and to switch on positive forces. I can suggest to patients that they are relaxed and can think more clearly and as they go more and more into a trance, the finger and thumb of their right hand will come together. Then, for example, I might suggest that they form a circle between the thumb and index finger. As they get more and more into a trance the finger and thumb can come together; their anxiety can become less and less until when they are actually touching there is no anxiety at all; they only have a feeling of comfort. That's a physical switch.

Another switch might be to suggest, "The right hand is held up in the air and as the hand lowers you become more relaxed; by the time it is resting on your lap you feel very comfortable." Focusing on the breathing as a switch allows inhalation to be connected with comfort and exhalation with getting rid of discomfort. The lowering of the hand is kind of a switch. The most common positive switch is just taking a deep breath, breathing in comfort and breathing out discomfort, breathing in peace and breathing out pain, and using the breathing as a switch. For most patients it's not even necessary to guide a patient into a trance before giving suggestions. That's why focus on breathing is often utilized in mediation or religion, to promote positive thinking and positive feeling.

***

How can I convey to you the spirit and some of the works of a man who was considered by many people to be the foremost therapeutic genius of our time? Just to state that he was a genius will certainly not impress anyone. To mention that 2,000 therapists from all over the world gathered for the first international congress honoring him, in December 1980, might intrigue some, might pique the curiosity of others, and might be dismissed by still others as just another indication that this man, whom they still confuse with Erik Erikson, was somewhat of a guru, who appealed to softminded thinkers.

Yet, when we run through some of the topics covered in the over 45 published papers from this congress (Zeig 1982), you may get some idea of the extent of Erickson's interests and influence. Of course, there were the expected papers on Erickson's contributions to hypnotherapy, to the treatment of depression, pain, and habit disorders. But there were also papers on "Erickson's Contribution to the Double Bind" and "Erickson's Contribution to the Interactional View of Psychotherapy," both from the Mental Research Institute of Palo Alto. It was also interesting to review "Erickson's Contributions to Family Therapy." In family therapy, his influence has been especially strong in the work of Jay Haley and through his contacts with Gregory Bateson, Paul Watzlawick, and others. In fact, he has been considered to be the "grandfather" of family therapy.

His contributions to anthropology were summarized at this congress by Madeleine Richeport (Richeport 1982, p. 372), who pointed out that "many anthropologists have benefited from Dr. Milton Erickson's commentary on their work with ritual trance, most notably Margaret Mead and Gregory Bateson in Bali, Jane Belo in Bali, Maya Deren in Haiti." The author credited Erickson with having guided her in her choice of areas of study, through the application of indirect suggestions. He also encouraged her to experience the phenomena that she was studying—mediumship, for example. She commented, "You cannot really learn about any trance without experiencing." This emphasis on experiencing is a key feature in Ericksonian approaches to psychotherapy and hypnosis. Indirect suggestion is another.

Paul Watzlawick, in another paper at this international congress (Watzlawick 1982) pointed out the following:

> As one reads his articles and books, one notices how he gradually moves from a strictly intrapsychic epistemology, based on traditional ideas of intrapsychic dynamics—from the allegedly curative value of insight and the monadic view of the skin-encapsulated human being as the ultimate unit of study—to a view that more and more took into account the social contexts in which human beings function or suffer.... I should imagine that long before family therapists became aware of the vicissitudes of change in human systems, Erickson had already discovered and utilized the almost incredible degree a patient's family and larger social context can help or hinder change.
> (p.147)

Watzlawick goes on to point out that

> this may not be everyone's view of Erickson's work or of hypnosis in general. We must not forget that hypnosis still plays the role of the fool or the court jester in the solemn halls of orthodoxy. The jester, as you remember, got away with undeniable truths precisely because he was a fool. He could be taken seriously only in a very selective way. Similarly, even today, hypnosis is seen by many as a somewhat outlandish way to further the aims of the true doctrine, namely, to lift suppressed material into consciousness. Once it has achieved that, it should hop along and no longer interfere with the promotion of insight.
> (p. 148)

Since Erickson tended to underemphasize the importance of insight, it might appear on the surface as if his approaches were not at all compatible with psychoanalytic ones. If this is at all true, it applies only to psychoanalytic approaches of 40 years ago.

I believe that most of my readers would tend to agree that insight is most likely to occur after a change rather than before. At least it can occur at any point in the circle of change and insight. Thus, in some ways, Erickson anticipated therapeutic approaches that were codified by neo-Freudians and other analysts.

Just as Karen Horney and other modern psychoanalysts had discovered that insight, by itself, does not necessarily lead to change, Erickson, who, perhaps because of his beginnings, working with hypnosis, was primarily interested in change, soon relegated insight to a relatively minor role. Instead, he emphasized a state of mind in which people were most open to change and learning and he called this state trance. His definitions of hypnosis varied over the years, but the last one that he used was, "Hypnosis is the evocation and utilization of unconscious learnings." He found many ways of inducing trance and of encouraging its development in patients, students and in himself.

Just as Horney analysts do not differentiate sharply between the "treatment" and other contacts with their patients—by telephone, during the greeting phase of a session, for example—Erickson started including therapeutic suggestions in the induction of trance. For example, if he was working with someone who was burdened by depression, he might use a hypnotic induction that involved arm levitation and might further encourage the idea of lightening by interspersing words such as light in his induction "patter." The patient and therapist together could then experience delight as they saw the light—sometimes as if it were a flash of lightning. He became a master of language, utilizing his early childhood experience of having had to read the dictionary from the very beginning in order to find a word that he was looking for. Incidentally, he was able to recall the exact moment, when, at age ten, he saw "a blinding, dazzling flash of light" and suddenly discovered alphabetical order. At that moment he learned how to use a dictionary and no longer needed to do such thorough reading to locate a word (Erickson 1977, p 49). He later learned that words, in all forms, even in corny puns, could be vehicles for promoting change and refocusing.

Since his approaches were always empirical (as Margaret Mead wrote (1977), "He never solved a problem in an old way if he could think of a new one and he usually could"), he seemed to have no clear-cut theoretical underpinning to his work. Others have tried recently to find such underpinnings and have extracted some of the elements that seem to be characteristically "Ericksonian." These include "prescribing the symptom," "encouraging a response by frustrating it," "using paradoxical imperatives," seeding ideas, "amplifying a deviation," and "providing a worse alternative" (Haley 1973).

Watzlawick has pointed out that most situations cannot be changed (Watzlawick 1982, p 153): "What can be changed, however, are the ways in which people conceptualize and try to come to terms with immutable facts." This had led to the idea of "reframing" and is a large element in Erickson's work.

Utilizing the patient's own language, not the language of any doctrine or "school," Erickson met the patient "where he is." Horney once said, "All we have to do to do analysis is be with the patient." Perhaps because Erickson was more of a visual person, his way of "being with" was more visual than the ways of many analysts who learn to "listen." He taught himself to become a master of the nonverbal.

My first contact with him occurred when I was 16 years old, living in London, Ontario. I was playing around with hypnosis with two friends. One day the two of them went to Eloise, Michigan, and when they returned, they brought with them tales of amazing experiences with this man, Milton Erickson, with whom they had spent an entire day. Imagine! He had the patience to spend an entire day with two adolescent boys! They told me that they had been in and out of trance all day long, that they would find themselves carrying out some act or other—opening a window, for example—and Erickson would then point out to them how he had directed them to do this—without words.

In spite of this early indirect contact with him, I did not meet Erickson personally until after I had completed my analytic training. After this meeting, in 1970, I published an article entitled, "Recent Experiences with Encounter, Gestalt, and Hypnotic Techniques" (Rosen, 1972). Later, Erickson asked me to write the foreword to his book, *Hypnotherapy: An Exploratory Casebook* (Erickson & Rossi, 1979). I wrote a chapter on Erickson's philosophy and values and presented it at the above-mentioned international congress (Rosen 1982). In 1982, I published *My Voice Will Go with You: The Teaching Tales of Milton H. Erickson.* Erickson had contracted as coauthor of this book but unfortunately died, in March 1980, leaving me to complete it.

In recent years, workers have attempted to extract from his complex and multileveled communications, some of the basic elements of his approach to therapy. Erickson, himself, summarized his basic approach to therapy as follows: "First you model the patient's world. Then you role-model the patient's world." He demonstrated that this modeling and role-modeling can be done verbally, nonverbally, and symbolically, as through the medium of metaphors (Rosen, 1982).

In spelling out the various phases of hypnotic induction, Ernest Rossi has noted (Erickson & Rossi, 1979, p. 8) that the first two phases involve a fixation of attention and the interruption of the usual mental set of the subject. Rossi called the latter step the "depotentiation of habitual frameworks and belief systems." The interruption may be achieved by simply asking a person to focus attention on something different from what he or she had been focusing on—numbers, a light, an inner sensation, even a pain. It may be achieved by evoking laughter or by a shock, confusion or surprise. Now, if we consider that a prime feature of all neurotic patterns and symptoms is, as Horney pointed out, their compulsivity, anything that can be used to interrupt or depotentiate these patterns or symptoms must be considered invaluable.

Simply entering into an altered state of consciousness, in itself, obviously interrupts the usual mental set of most people. If this altered state of consciousness is tied in with something constructive, instead of being tied to compulsive symptoms, the constructive pattern may be self-reinforcing. For example, with compulsive eaters, the sight of food may become associated with an entirely new mental set, in which the person is concerned about and aware of his health, physical appearance, and so on. When he finds that he does not have to eat, he acquires a feeling of mastery. This feeling of mastery makes him feel better about himself, and thus it becomes easier for him to carry out other activities that are self-esteem building. The usual mental set, in which the compulsive eater is entranced at the sight and thought of food, the one in which he is "stimulus bound," is replaced with a set in which he has a choice about eating.

We realize that there is a vast difference between being able to interrupt a set temporarily and being able to do it on a long-term basis. Some of Erickson's genius lay in his being able to use the phenomena of posthypnotic suggestions, interspersing these suggestions so that, later, they would be reactivated by cues or by events and stimuli which would inevitably occur in a person's life. The following account, "Dry Beds" (Rosen, 1982, p. 113), illustrates this.

Dry Beds

As in Sufi tales or Zen stories, the recipient of the knowledge of the healer must be in a state of readiness to receive. In many of those stories the supplicant comes to the master but is refused entry until "the vehicle is ready to receive the riches of the teaching." Erickson often accomplishes this preparation by causing the listener or the patient to wait a long time before he delivers his "punch line." For example, when he presented the next tale to a group of students, he spent about one-half hour in building up to the final prescription. Some of this time was spent in outlining the background history. Some was spent in asking the listeners how they would treat such a patient. Some time was spent in telling other stories, not directly related to the problem. He repeated such phrases as "There is something that you know but don't know that you know. When you know what it is that you don't know you know, then you will be able to have a permanently dry bed." This type of puzzling and yet intriguing statement causes the listeners to do what Ernest Rossi has called an "inner search." The listener is thus already beginning to search inside himself for resources that may help in the healing process. When we consider one of Erickson's induction techniques, the "waiting technique," the same principle applies. The patient literally is left begging for more. Then he is ready to receive.

> A mother brought her eleven-year-old daughter in to see me. As soon as I heard about her bed-wetting, I sent the mother out of the room with the belief that the girl could tell me her story. The girl told me that she had a bladder infection in very early infancy, that she was treated by an urologist, and that the infection had persisted for five or six years, maybe longer. She had been cystoscoped regularly, hundreds of times, and eventually the focus

of the infection was found in one kidney. That had been removed and she had been free of infections for about four years. She had been cystoscoped so many hundreds of times, and her bladder and sphincter were so stretched, that she wet the bed every night, as soon as her bladder relaxed in her sleep. During the day she could forcibly control her bladder, unless she laughed. The relaxation that goes with laughter caused her to wet her pants.

Her parents thought that since she had had her kidney removed and had been free of the infection for several years, she ought to learn to control herself. She had three younger sisters, who called her bad names and ridiculed her. All of the mothers knew that she wet her bed. And all the schoolchildren, two or three thousand of them, knew that she was a bed wetter and that she wet her pants when she laughed. So, she was the butt of much ridicule.

She was very tall, very pretty, blond, with long hair that reached down to her waist. She was really a very charming girl. She was ostracized, ridiculed; more was demanded of her than she could produce. She had to endure the pity of neighbors and the ridicule of her sisters and the schoolchildren. She couldn't go to slumber parties or spend the night with relatives because of her bed-wetting. I asked her if she had seen any other doctors. She said that she had seen a lot of them, had swallowed a barrel full of pills and a barrel full of medicine, and nothing helped.

I told her that I was like all the other doctors. I couldn't help her either. "But you already know something but you don't know that you know it. As soon as you find out what it is that you already know and don't know that you know, you can begin having a dry bed."

Then I told her, "I am going to ask you a very simple question and I want a very simple answer. Now, here's the question. If you were sitting in the bathroom, urinating, and a strange man poked his head in the doorway, what would you do?"

"I'd freeze!"

That's right. You'd freeze—and stop urinating. Now, you know what you already knew, but didn't know that you already knew it. Namely, that you can stop urinating at any time for any stimulus you choose. You really don't need a strange man poking his head in the bathroom. Just the idea of it is enough. You'll stop. You'll freeze. And when he goes away you will start urinating.

"Now, having a dry bed is a very difficult job. You might have your first dry bed in two weeks. And there has to be a lot of practice, starting and stopping. Some days you may forget to practice starting and stopping. That's all right. Your body will be good to you. It will always give you further opportunities. And some days you may be too busy to practice starting and stopping, but that's all right. Your body will always give you opportunities to start and stop. It would surprise me very much if you had a permanently dry bed within three months. It would also surprise me if you didn't have a permanently dry bed within six months. And the first dry bed will be much easier than two dry beds in succession. And three dry beds in succession is much harder. And four dry beds in succession is still harder. After that it gets easier. You can have five, six, seven, a whole week of dry beds. And then you can know that you can have one week of dry beds and another week of dry beds."

I took my time with the girl. I had nothing else to do. I spent an hour and a half with her and dismissed her. About two weeks later she brought in this present for me—the first present she had ever given with the knowledge that she had had a dry bed (it was a knitted purple cow). I value that present. And six months later she was staying overnight at friends', relatives', at slumber parties, in a hotel. Because it is the patient who does the therapy. I didn't think it was the family that needed therapy, even though the parents were impatient, the sisters called her bad names, the schoolchildren ridiculed her. My feeling was that her parents would have to adjust to her dry beds. So would her sisters and the schoolchildren—and the neighbors. In fact, I saw no other course for them. I didn't think it was necessary to explain anything to the father, the mother, the sisters, or anybody else. I had told her what she already knew but didn't know that she knew.

And all of you have grown up with the idea that when you empty your bladder you empty it all the way. And you assume that. The important thing is that all of you have had the experience of being interrupted and shutting off a stream of urine very suddenly. Everybody has that experience—and she had forgotten it. All I did was remind her of something she already knew but she didn't know she knew it.

In other words, in doing therapy you regard your patient as an individual and no matter how much of a problem her bed-wetting was to her parents, her sisters, neighbors and school children, it was primarily her problem. And all she needed to know was something she already knew—and the therapy for all the others was letting them make their own adjustments.

Psychotherapy should be an orientation to the patient and an orientation to the primary problem itself. And remember this. That all of us have our individual language, and that when you listen to a patient, you should listen knowing that he is speaking an alien language and that you should not try to understand in terms of your language. Understand the patient in his language.

This is one of my favorite Erickson tales, perhaps because Erickson would almost always introduce it with a comment such as "You will be especially interested in this story, Sid." I puzzled for a long time before I could find his message to me and finally was able to extract two main ones.

The first is that I can learn control of thoughts, of working energies, and of symptoms, such as anxiety. I must do this, however, not by willpower, but by discovering which stimuli are necessary to induce me to "start and stop." Then I must take the opportunities to practice "starting and stopping."

The second message is that "all of you have grown up with the idea that when you empty your bladder, you empty it all the way." In the version of this tale that was published in *A Teaching Seminar with Milton H. Erickson*, edited by Jeffrey Zeig, Erickson added some extra sentences that make this second point even clearer. "All she needed to know was that she could stop her urination at any time, with the right stimulus." We grow up thinking that we have got to finish, but that isn't true. I have found this attitude to be a great help in accomplishing such tasks as writing. The coercive feeling that we must finish can easily block spontaneity and creativity. A far more effective way of getting something done is by "starting and stopping," according to one's inner rhythm. I have found this story to be effective in helping patients overcome blockages, such as writers block.

Erickson encouraged his patients and his students to trust their unconscious minds. He really believed that we have the capacity to solve our own dilemmas and problems and that, with some encouragement and support, this capacity will be utilized. He taught us, as therapists, to utilize whatever our patients bring to us. We ought to convey the attitude that whatever they bring is all right. There is no need to work through resistance—or even to consider any behavior as resistance. He would encourage us to find something, even in the most obnoxious or pathological behavior, which could be reframed, redirected, and utilized for constructive ends.

A classical example of this was the woman who had a large gap between her front teeth, which she felt made her very ugly. She also could not establish any relationships with men, and it appeared that she would never marry. As described in *Uncommon Therapy* (Haley, 1973), Erickson elicited the fact that there was a water cooler in her office and that there was a young man whom she would regularly see there. Neither she nor the man had the nerve to talk to one another. He suggested that she practice learning to squirt water through her teeth. After she had learned to do this well, he had her do this near the water cooler, squirting the water in the face of the young man. The young man was surprised, reacted in a playful way, by saying something like, "You little vixen," and she then, following Erickson's instructions, ran away from him. In the manner of swains through the ages, he ran after her and finally caught her, giving her a big hug and a kiss. As in many Erickson tales, they were married soon afterward and had several children.

When this story was published in *Uncommon Therapy*, *Time* magazine made fun of it, entirely missing the point. Although we may use complicated language and concepts in examining his concepts, Erickson's real genius lay in utilizing, as in this case, whatever a patient brought to him, and in encouraging people to treasure whatever they were given by life and fate.

Of course, he modeled this philosophy, as I have illustrated in his "teaching tale," "Learning to Stand Up" (Rosen, 1982, p. 47). Here he said:

> We learn so much at a conscious level, and then we forget what we learn, and use the skill. You see, I had a terrific advantage over others. I had polio, and I was totally paralyzed, and the inflammation was so great that I had a sensory paralysis too. I could move my eyes and my hearing was undisturbed. I got very lonesome lying in bed, unable to move anything except my eyeballs. I was quarantined on the farm with seven sisters, one brother, two parents, and a practical nurse. How could I entertain myself? I started watching people in my environment. I soon learned that my sisters could say, "No", when they meant, "Yes." And they could say "Yes" and mean "No" at the same time. They could offer another sister an apple and hold it back, and I began studying nonverbal language and body language.

His study of all kinds of language continued throughout a career of over 50 years. Just as he did with my friends, he studied everyone with whom he had contact. Everyone, not only his patients, but friends, family, and colleagues, were subjects for him.

It is paradoxical that hypnosis, which is still seen by most analysts as the most directive therapy, is, in Ericksonian approaches at least, one of the most interactive therapies that exist today. Addressing the American Psychoanalytic Association several years ago, Lawrence Kubie pointed out that a person enters into a trance state not as the result of suggestions, but that he becomes more open to suggestions as a result of being in a trance. Once he is in that state, the barrier that normally separates one of us from another is dissolved and the "subject" or "patient" hears the "hypnotist's" voice as if it were his own and responds to it accordingly. This accounts for the fact that a hypnotized person will only follow suggestions that are ego-syntonic.

The breaking down of the barrier works in both directions, and the therapist who allows himself to enter into a trance state is not only in closer touch with his own unconscious but more open than usual to communications from his patient. In fact, one of the difficulties of working in this modality is the experience of literally feeling a patient's pain—physical and emotional—very intensely at times. Still, I would encourage therapists to use self-hypnosis deliberately (I know that you enter into trances accidentally) in order to be the most effective in your work.

Again, this approach is not unique to Erickson. One of my favorite supervisors, Isidore Portnoy, advised me to "Listen to your own responses during sessions. Listen to even a tingling in your little toe." The advantage of deliberately entering into a trance state or, at least, of recognizing when one is in a trance state, is, in my opinion, that one is likely to have more awareness of these inner signals or messages to oneself than one might otherwise have.

Let me tell you about a recent situation in which I trusted my own unconscious, often working in a trance state myself. I had been treating a 32-year-old psychologist who had suffered severe agoraphobic symptoms for several years. I had helped her to discover that, like many phobics, she was hypersuggestible. I had reframed this tendency as a skill, a capacity that she could utilize, not only to alleviate her symptoms, but even to help in focusing on goals, in concentrating, and in changing her own mood, all through autosuggestion.

After her symptoms had been in remission for over two years, she underwent a relapse. Her father had become ill, and a supervisor, whom she had identified with her father, was about to leave the hospital where she worked. She came in feeling suicidal, having hardly eaten for several weeks, looking gaunt and skeletal and stating that her agoraphobic symptoms had returned. She was hypnotized, was reminded about her skill in self-hypnosis, and was asked to open her eyes and describe what she saw. She described only blackness, dark areas in the room. I suggested that she could change these perceptions, that she could plant a flower in the dark area under the couch, that she could bring a ray of sunlight into that area. Gradually she was encouraged to hallucinate a yellow color over everything. She associated yellow with a rise in her mood. Her mood actually improved tremendously, and she was then able to say, "I really feel like having a good cry. I haven't cried since I heard that A was leaving." Before her next session she had started to eat again and was able to tolerate some of the symptoms that she had, such as a feeling of depersonalization. I was then able to help her discover that she could change these symptoms.

In order to model a more accepting attitude toward symptoms, I told her Erickson's story about his having awakened in a strange hotel room, opening his right eye and not knowing where he was. He had thought to himself, "I wonder what would happen if I opened my left eye." He had then closed his right eye and opened his left eye-and he knew where he was! He had closed his left eye again and opened his right eye and, once more, he did not know where he was! In telling this story he was modeling an attitude of curiosity, of wonder, about symptoms that might have frightened other people.

She responded very positively to the indirect suggestion, as conveyed in this tale, that it was all right to have unusual perceptions, such as feelings of unreality and that one could change one's responses by assuming an attitude of "wondering" rather than one of fear.

My choice of interventions, those described above and others, was made, mostly unconsciously, in the "therapeutic trance state" in which I often work, especially when I am most effective.

Another patient, whom I saw recently, was a 19-year-old college freshman who had returned home for his Christmas break. Just prior to his return he had written his parents that he would not be able to continue in school. He had stated in that letter,

> I don't picture myself with a future. I find no meaning in my life. I find myself to be an observer of myself, wondering what I am going to do next. I

am like a spectator in my own life. I could not choose courses of action. I can only wonder and predict.

He had been told that if he did not have a certain paper completed by January 4 and mailed in as of that date he would not be readmitted for the next term at college. Although he was an excellent writer, he was unable to get himself to write anything. He had always obtained good marks because, on the occasions when he had written something, it had turned out to be so outstanding that his teachers knew that he could write.

I hypnotized him and, in a trance state, reviewed his past history, which I knew included a period of three years during his early teens when he had been successfully treated for a histiocytic lymphoma. He had had previous psychotherapy for over one year, during which he had developed a rather good understanding of the connections between his feelings of meaninglessness and hopelessness and the fact that he had almost died from this cancer. He had understood that he had been living for the purpose of pleasing his parents, and so on.

In my sessions with him, however, I did not focus on understanding his feelings of despair or the causes of his "writing block." Instead, in the trance state, I gave him general suggestions, such as the following: "I'd be very surprised if you developed some enlightenment within one week. I'd be even more surprised if you did not develop some enlightenment within two weeks." I gave him this suggestion on December 23 and followed it with other interventions within the next two weeks. On January 4 he had mailed his completed paper. He returned to school, and his father, who was also my patient, told me that he had returned with a completely changed attitude—without blockages or obsessive self-doubting.

What had I done? What had I said to him?

In addition to guiding him toward his own inner wisdom, I had given him suggestions on different levels. For example, I had told him, "You have a right to be right and to write." I had also suggested that "anything worth doing is worth doing poorly." In fact, I had directed him to write a poor paper before the deadline date, to make a great effort to make sure that this paper was poorly done—but that it would be done. I had projected him into the future and had him see himself ten years hence with different scenarios. In one of them he had dropped out of school and in another he had completed his schooling. He had definitely preferred the second one.

After he had been able to write the paper, he was then able to look back and recall that, when he had written his first English paper, in seventh grade, he had been given a mark of only B+. His teacher had been a pretty young woman, and he had had a crush on her. He had been very upset at receiving only a B+ from her and had said to her, "Congratulations. You have just given me my first grade under an A." His hurt pride had led him, after that time, into great difficulty in producing anything in writing.

We could analyze his reasons for not being able to work in many different frameworks—in terms of family dynamics, Horneyian concepts of idealized image, neurotic pride, and so on. But my purpose had been to get him to be able to simply do something, if he wanted to. He could then look back and understand the reasons why he had not been able to do something up to that point. And he had succeeded. Incidentally, the paper that he wrote, and of which I have a copy, was related only very loosely to the topic that he had been studying. He had literally followed my suggestion to write just anything. Actually, he had produced an autobiographical study, of about 15 pages, on the subject of how people are rendered powerless and dependent by forces beyond their control. He had related this to inside oppressors and to the injustice of such things. Actually, he had written a clinical study of his own development of learning and writing blocks and of their cure. For example, he had referred to my treatment of him. "Since I have been home." he wrote,

> I have been seeing a new type of therapist, a hypnotist. In our first three sessions nothing worked. Then, in our last session, the doctor forced a decision. Reasoning that the pain inherent in the consequences of not writing was insufficiently intense to change my status quo, he elevated my pain. While I sat in a hypnotic trance, he suggested that I not relax, that I increase the pain 100 times. That day I was miserable. At night I hardly slept, plagued by nightmares. The following afternoon I decided to write this paper.

Erickson's definition of hypnosis—"The evocation and utilization of unconscious learnings"—might sound to my readers very much like their own definition of psychoanalytic therapy. Perhaps, when therapy is effective, there is no difference between the two. In that case, we would say that the only difference between Erickson's approaches and that of most Horney analysts, at least, would be in his development of original methods of evoking and utilizing these unconscious learnings. He took much more responsibility than most therapists for the conducting of the therapy, yet he stated "most therapists feel that they must control the therapy. I believe that therapy is like a snowball rolling down a mountain. It can grow into an avalanche. And all the therapist has to do is start the snowball rolling." He also stated,

> Direct suggestion ... does not evoke the re-association and reorganization of ideas, understandings and memories so essential for an actual cure.... Effective results in hypnotic psychotherapy ... derive only from the patient's activities. The therapist merely stimulates the patient into activity, often not knowing what that activity may be. And then he guides the patient and exercises clinical judgment in determining the amount of work to be done to achieve the desired result.
>
> *(Rosen, 1973)*

From studying the many case reports which he published and from watching him work, it appears clear to me that he demanded and evoked much less "doctrinal compliance" than most therapists. And yet he was recognized as a master manipulator. This is a typical Ericksonian paradox: the master manipulator allowed and stimulated the greatest freedom! (Rosen, 1973)

Note

1 This chapter was previously published in the *American Journal of Psychoanalysis* 1984, Vol 44(2), pp. 133–145.

References

Erickson, M.H. (1977). Autohypnotic Experiences of M. H. Erickson. *American Journal of Clinical Hypnosis*, 20(1): 36–54.

Erickson, M.H., and Rossi, E.L. (1979). *Hypnotherapy: An Exploratory Casebook*. New York: Irvington.

Haley, J. (1973). *Uncommon Therapy: The Psychiatric Techniques of Milton H. Erickson, M.D.* New York: W. W. Norton

Mead, M. (1977). The Originality of Milton Erickson. *American Journal of Clinical Hypnosis*, 20(1): 4–5.

Richeport, M. (1982). Erickson's Contributions to Anthropology. In J. Zeig (ed.), *Ericksonian Approaches to Hypnosis and Psychotherapy*. New York: Brunner/Mazel.

Rosen, S. (1972). Recent Experiences with Encounter, Gestalt, And Hypnotic Techniques. *American Journal Psychoanalysis*, 32(1): 90–105.

Rosen, S. (1973). Foreword. In M.H. Erickson, and E.L. Rossi, *Hypnotherapy: An Exploratory Casebook*. New York: W. W. Norton,

Rosen, S. (1982). *My Voice Will Go with You: The Teaching Tales of Milton H. Erickson*. New York: Norton.

Rosen, S. (1982). The Values and Philosophy of Milton H. Erickson. In J. Zeig (ed.), *Ericksonian Approaches to Hypnosis and Psychotherapy*, pp. 462–476. New York: Brunner/Mazel.

Watzlawick, P. (1982). Erickson's Contribution to the Interactional View of Psychotherapy. In J. Zeig (ed.), *Ericksonian Approaches to Hypnosis and Psychotherapy*, pp. 147–148. New York: Brunner/Mazel.

Zeig, J. (ed.) (1982). *Ericksonian Approaches to Hypnosis and Psychotherapy*. New York: Brunner/Mazel.

6

HYPNOSIS AS AN ADJUNCT TO CHEMOTHERAPY IN CANCER[1]

Introduction

What is the goal of hypnotic interventions in patients who have terminal cancer diagnoses?

One goal is to enable them to go through the treatment of the cancer with minimum number of side effects. How do I do this? I play with time and I have patients experience having gone through the chemotherapy with minimum number of side effects.

Another goal is to give patients a feeling of hope and a sense of mastery which most of them have lost. They find themselves feeling very ill from the chemotherapy. A sense of mastery is a sense of going through chemotherapy, with a minimum degree of side effects, such as nausea, which can lead patients to prefer a speedy death to the sense of being tortured by pain.

Hypnosis can also open up unconscious learnings, such as what it feels like to be free of symptoms and to see the treatment as a help rather than as some kind of experience that is like subjugation to chemical attacks.

For example, in treating one patient who saw cancer as associated with contamination, I sought to have her see the letter "C" associated not with negatives—cancer, contamination and chemotherapy. Instead I sought to have the letter "C" associate with corrective images, such as "clean, clear, celestial, comforting." In other words, I replaced bad Cs with good Cs in her associations. It's a form of concretizing and switching.

Or there's the patient who was very much involved with music. I had her associate music as being a "healing music." In terminal cases, I encourage people who believe in the afterlife, or reincarnation, or living on through their children and their work to do so.

In my experience, hypnotic intervention can be more effective than marijuana, especially when directed to the comfort and development of the whole person. I use time distortion to have patients seeing themselves at a purer age, looking back and having had suffered with cancer at some time in the past. The goal is not to cure the patient but to give her experience of being at least free of the side effects of the chemotherapy. The goal is to increase the association of the chemotherapy with healing, which of course is its purpose, and to minimize the negative side effects. The cancer patient is guided to experience herself at a later time, several years into the future, having been successfully treated for her symptoms.

With hypnosis, the feeling of diminution of anxiety, and the sense of mastery, is coming from the patient herself, not from some external agent, like drugs. And that sense of mastery could become more pervasive throughout the day rather than in response to an external stimulation.

The goal is for patients to engage in self-hypnosis rather than only at the suggestion of a therapist. When patients experience the mastery of hypnotizing themselves, the images that are invoked in a hypnotic state are positive images not negative ones, and they can change a patient's entire experience of reality. For example, feelings of anticipatory nausea can be replaced by feelings of comfort or images of enjoying a meal.

In some cases, these therapies can prolong life. Consider the daughter who told me her mother had been calmer and more content in her last year than ever before. The daughter attributed her mother's sense of peace to psychotherapy.

***

Patients who are undergoing chemotherapy for cancer sometimes feel that the side effects of the chemotherapy are so uncomfortable that they would opt for a speedy death rather than endure the "extra torture." Several investigators have reported that the side effects can be ameliorated by the use of marijuana and behavioral desensitization (Morrow & Morrell, 1982). In my experience, and that of others, hypnotic intervention can more helpful than these other approaches, especially when they are directed toward the comfort and development of the whole person (Redd, Rosenberger, & Hendler, 1982–1983).

From my first contact with a patient with cancer I utilize approaches such as projection into the future. In a trance state I guide patients to see themselves at a mature age, perhaps in their eighties, looking back upon this period of time, when they *had* suffered with cancer. They can see not only that they learned to survive physically but that they went through the chemotherapy treatment, comfortably and safely and had grown and learned from the entire experience. I usually include both general suggestions, aimed at encouraging learning, comfort and healing, and specific ones, aimed at symptoms such as nausea.

After an Early Learning Set induction, I may say:

> You can become a bodiless mind. And as a bodiless mind you can travel anywhere at all in time or in space. You can be three years old, or 10 years old. You can enjoy comfort at any age.

(Sometimes I will have the patients signal to me, with automatic movements, when they are comfortable.)

Then I may suggest

> Today's date is not 1983. Today is not July 18, 1983. And you are not in New York City, in Dr. Rosen's office. This is 1993. And I don't know where you are. You could be at home. You could be on a vacation trip. You could be with friend, your children, your grandchildren. I don't know where you are, or what you are doing. But you are comfortable, aren't you? You do feel good, don't you?

Case Example

After I get a positive response to age progression I may go even further into the future. For example, with one hospitalized woman, age 43, who had both breasts removed, I said during my first contact with her:

> You are 80 years old—83 years old. And you can look back 40 years, seeing yourself at age 43. And you can realize that the period around age 43 was really a very important time in your life—a watershed, the time when you really began to understand the meaning of your life, the value of your life. A very important time for you. You can't say that you were actually lucky to have gotten cancer but, in a way, you feel that it was lucky for you.

I will then play with time:

> You are age 83, looking back at you yourself at age 43. And you see what happened after you saw Dr. Rosen. How did you go through that period? How did you go through the chemotherapy? Was the chemotherapy upsetting to you? Did it take one week, did it take two weeks after you saw Dr. Rosen, before the chemotherapy was accepted as a matter-of-fact treatment? As a helper? Or did it take only one session before you felt better? Did it take a month? Two weeks?

As I offer different times, I watch for responses and note them. Then I progress the patient, in the same way as I might bring her back from an early childhood regression.

> And that young woman of 43 grows older, hour by hour, day by day, week by week, month by month, year by year—and really enjoys her life, doesn't

she? Life has become very meaningful. She appreciates the value of every moment. Of course, as Longfellow said, "Into each life some rain must fall, some days must be dark and dreary." There were sometimes when things were not so hot. There were times when you thought that you were not going to be able to make it, to get through another hour, another day. But you got through those times, didn't you (again looking back from age 83)?

Discussion

After the general approach, outlined above, I might have the patient hypnotically review the entire chemotherapy treatment, using imagery, when possible. The progression into the future has three possible effects:

1. It implies that the person will survive and thereby adds to a sense of hope. Hope has been associated with greater survival rates and greater longevity (Newton, 1982, p 112).
2. It is an indirect way of requesting the unconscious mind to devise ways of dealing with the side effects of therapy and with the psychological and physiological impact of the cancer.
3. Patients are left with some sense of mastery and a feeling of process as they preview responses over the immediate future and through the next few months of therapy.

When we consider the reported results of the Simontons and Creighton (Simonton, Simonton, & Creighton, 1978), and Hall (Hall, 1982), in which it appears that the use of imagery or hypnotic and self-hypnotic approaches may prolong the life of cancer patients, it is possibly negligent *not* to make the approaches available to all cancer patients.

Developing Treatment Approaches

What specific suggestions do I give to a patient undergoing chemotherapy? I keep in mind Erickson's advice.

> Maladies, whether psychogenic or organic, follow definite patterns of some sort ... a disruption of this pattern could be a most therapeutic measure; it often matters little how small the disruption was, if introduced early enough.
> *(Erickson, 1980, p. 254)*

Details of the patient's response to chemotherapy to date can provide directions for treatment, for example, to a patient who reported the development of nausea about two hours after receiving intravenous chemotherapy, I suggested that, about two hours after the treatment, he could feel comfortable or he could sleep for two hours. If the situation was not one in which he could sleep, I would utilize time distortion, so that he could experience the feeling of having slept for several hours, even though the experience would take place during only a few minutes of clock time. He could rest his head on his office desk for two minutes, which could be experienced as several hours of sleep. On awakening from this "sleep," the patient could then have a feeling of hunger, with the understanding that hunger is the best antidote to nausea.

If patients have not had chemotherapy previously, their expectancy of sickness derives from stories they heard or read or from suggestions received from nurses or physicians. It is remarkable how specific treatment personnel can be in suggesting side effects. One patient was told, for example, "You will probably be O. K. for the first two treatments, but most people get very sick by the third treatment, from the cumulative effect of the medication."

It is often necessary to counteract these "helpful" suggestions. For example, I explain to patients the nature of indirect suggestions, so that they can be alerted to them. Then, I make counter suggestions, such as, "You ought to get an increasing feeling of well-being and security as you realize that you have received an adequate dose of medication, perhaps after your third or fourth treatment."

Anticipatory nausea, a well-known phenomenon, is most obviously "purely psychological" in origin. An example is the patient who becomes violently nauseated on accidentally looking at a dressing gown worn in the hospital during chemotherapy. This type of nausea is easiest to treat. Simple desensitization, using visualizations, can be employed. For example, patients can visualize themselves in a comfortable situation, eating an enjoying a meal. Then while maintaining the comfortable feeling, they can see and feel themselves looking at the robe. Later they can visualize or think of themselves as walking down the street towards the doctor's office for the therapy session, feeling comfortable and looking forward to the treatment.

Self-hypnosis can be taught to supplement therapeutic suggestions. Audiotapes, custom-made in the presence of the patient, can be helpful as a supplement, or can replace self-hypnosis in some patient. Because these tapes may be used before going to sleep at night, I often include sleep-promoting suggestion and suggestions for healing dreams.

Physiological responses to chemotherapy can be altered by the use of indirect or metaphorical suggestions. For example, I have decreased intestinal cramping and diarrhea by encouraging a patient to visualize a running stream which moved roughly at times and calmly at other times, with increasing periods of calm until it formed a tranquil pool.

Changing Patient Attitudes

The best way to change a fearful attitude towards chemotherapy is to intervene in ways that minimize discomfort. However, it is sometimes helpful to address attitudes directly, to correct historical misconceptions and to present the therapy in a positive light. Using patients' values and conceptions is a principal technique of the Ericksonian method.

For example, one patient was initially angry at the chemotherapy. She said, "I feel I'm just poisoning my body. The same way I did when I was seven years old and had X-ray treatment on my thymus." I reframed the situation and helped her see the chemotherapy as strengthening the defensive forces in her body, so that they could destroy the already poisoned, or potentially poisoned cancer processes.

Another patient who already saw chemotherapy as one of her "allies" conceived cancer as being "dirty." In working with her, chemotherapy and cleansing were repeatedly connected and associated.

For those patients who develop phobic responses to the chemotherapy, or to taking oral medication between intravenous treatments, therapy often can be quite simple. One successful method I have used is to have the patient practice visualizing swallowing the pills in a matter-of-fact manner.

Especially in cases which appear to be terminal I determine in which areas patients can find hope, whether it be through hope of magical recovery, through ideas of an afterlife or reincarnation, or simply through the thought of living on through their children or their work. Looking forward to peace and the end of trouble may be relieving to some people.

Approaches to Hypnotic Induction

Induction techniques depend on what is available to the therapist and on the responsiveness of the patient. Healing suggestions often are incorporated into the induction. For example, with an arm levitation induction, I may casually mention, "It feels good, doesn't it, to be lighter? And, as your arm goes up, you can raise your sights; you can go beyond yourself, you look forward to periods of increasing enlightenment."

Case Example

One 63-year-old patient had undergone a radical mastectomy and was soon to begin chemotherapy. She was referred to me two years previously because of anxiety and fears that she *might* develop cancer. She associated her cancer with a type of dirtiness, contamination. In fact, she felt that the letter "c" generally referred to negatives "cancer, calamity, contamination, crud, and, of course, chemotherapy." In the following induction it can be seen that posthypnotic suggestions, for healing in general, for comfort and specifically for minimal aide effects from chemotherapy are included from the beginning.

Alter a confusion-type induction; she was presented with time-distortion and disorienting suggestions:

> You know that St. Patrick's Day came last year and that it probably rained, as it always seems to do on St. Patrick's, Day, this year, in 1981, just as it will in

1982 and as it did in 1979. You know that, a year or so ago, back in 1980, you were impelled to call Dr. Rosen, hoping that working with him would help you in dealing with some severe anxieties. When he didn't answer the telephone, you decided that it wasn't the right time to do this. You don't know now, that two years from today you will actually be seeing Dr. Rosen, after some of your worst fears have materialized. You have a lot of conscious awareness of the importance of fantasy, the importance of listening to your own unconsciousness mind. When you do see Dr. Rosen, in March of 1982, you will want to be prepared to use whatever you have learned throughout your life so that you can redirect not only your conscious thoughts, but your unconscious activity as well. You can do this by tapping that vast reservoir of unconscious learnings and extracting from it some of the most positive, the most helpful, the most creative experiences and moments. You can find yourself inspired, when the occasion arises, to lift yourself above yourself, or to take yourself outside of yourself, at times, or to go inside of yourself, in order to oversee or to direct those powerful healing forces which you know are present. You don't have to force those forces.

You don't have to force yourself to concentrate. All you need to do is make gentle requests of your unconscious mind. "I would like to ask my unconscious mind to help me to go through this experience comfortably and effectively." Once you have made that request you can let yourself go into a deeper trance, knowing that you have all the resources that you need. You can call on resources from inside and from outside—from your friends. You can allow them to nurture you, temporarily, putting aside your pride for a while, the feeling that you have to take care of everything, for yourself and for others. You can allow yourself to be sick, for a while, not needing to feel sick, but knowing that there is a cleaning up job to be done there, and that it will be done, as efficiently, as effectively and as comfortably as possible.

You know, deep down inside, do you not, that this will be done. It is not just a wish fulfillment, is it? You are going to be well very soon, are you not? I'm waiting for a signal. Yes! Like that! If you are wondering if that is just a wish fulfillment, that you are deliberately moving that thumb, try to stop it from going up, finding that the more you try to stop it the higher up it wants to go. That's right! Like that!

You can sense that force that is working inside you now. And that unconscious force that is working against you, too, can you not? That last force will become weaker and weaker as you become stronger.

You can have some understanding now of the question that was asked a long time ago. "What is the source of this unconscious part of you that is working against you now?" You can talk in words and tell me about it, if you like. (Patient: The source is fear. But it's not going to win—because fear is no good.)

Can you take that fear and wrap it up? Where is it located—in your left hand? Rather than try to fight against it, can you dispense with it, in some other way? Right now, when your hand becomes clenched so tightly, you can try to hold that fear in. The fingers and joints become locked tight. If you try to open that fist, the more you try to open it the tighter the fingers clench. That's right. Try to open it, finding that you can't. That's right. You can really feel the tightness, the tension. Locate all the tightness, all the tension from your body into that left hand; all of the despair. [A loud car horn is heard, persistently blowing outside the window.] And that damned irritating horn can make you feel more frustrated and angry, can't it—till you feel like smashing something—with that left fist ... And when you've had so much of it as you can stand for now ... yes, let it build up further ... there are times... when we are in severe pain, that we naturally and instinctively hold on to something, just as you are holding on now ... in that left fist ... until the fist itself becomes painful ... the hand becomes achy ... When you don't want to stand it for another moment, just nod your head, once.... Now lean back and take a deep breath, and let the fist relax and open, letting out the fear, letting out the tension. Letting it out of your body. Letting it leave your mind... like that ... yes ...

You focus on your breathing for a moment or two, letting yourself go into a more relaxed state, a deeper trance. Enter into your cocoon ... and you are not alone here. You become more ... and more relaxed ... and as you relax more and more, you can listen to your unconscious messages ... You've heard the negative ones. You have seen them ... in your dream ... but you can tune up the positive messages now, too ... so that they become not only messages from your conscious mind, not only the grim determination of a very strong woman, to overcome this illness ... it will become a voice from a very, very deep source, which just quietly knows that you will become well ... and safe ... and able to proceed with the living of your life again ... very, very soon.

I don't know what images are going to come to you ... to represent this very positive feeling ... but I do know that you will come up with some images that are meaningful to you ... corrective images, clean, clear, perhaps celestial ... certainly comforting. [Note the "good Cs."] Can you see them, or hear them now? (Patient shakes her head "no.") Would you like me to supply some? All right.... You have a vast repertoire of music ... much vaster than mine. I do not want to limit you. You could think of "The Ode to Joy" ... or a Schubert Mass ... or even some Mozart.... Just scan through your repertoire ... until you hit on some small piece of music that you can sense is a healing music for you. You can hear that, in your mind, more and more vividly, more and more clearly. You can see the orchestra. You can pick out various parts of the orchestra.... So, you will remember these and they will come back automatically. And they can be so vivid and so clear that you will be not quite sure—is there really an orchestra, or is it a record that I hear, or is it just in my own head? And it really doesn't matter. All that matters is that you know that you're creative, your healing forces are liberated, more and more ...

You can go into a deeper trance and can take a look into your future, if you like. You are with your family, your husband, and everything is back to normal, isn't it?

Or, are you involved in newer projects that interest you? I [your husband] is well, is he not? You had fears, back in 1982, that he might not be. And he is 74 years old now, isn't he? No? How old is he? (Patient: 72.) Yes, but now it's 1984. He's 74. Can you see him being well this year? And you are just a youngster—10 years younger.

And that chemotherapy is behind you. And that is a relief, isn't it? (Patient: Yes.) How did you go through it? Was it uncomfortable for you? Or were you able to utilize some of the things that you were working on with Dr. Rosen and others, to make it more comfortable? Did your hair fall out? That was not a serious problem, anyway, was it? You had the wig—a whole series of them, if you needed them.... And what about the nausea that people talk about? Did you have much nausea? Or were you able to just take a deep breath, whenever you felt it beginning, and let that feeling go out of you ... blow it out ... instead of having to throw it up ... remembering that then was a desire at one time to want to throw something up, in despair, wasn't there? Were you able to let go of that despair, in some other way? ... to focus on feeling relaxed and comfortable ... and safe ... during the treatment and after the treatment? (Patient nods "yes.")

This patient was seen for hypnotherapy and psychotherapy once or twice a week for about eight months. She completed her first series of chemotherapy treatments with no nausea or vomiting and a minimal amount of weakness. Periods of depression and anxiety were very brief, lasting for only hours. She maintained an active social and family life, philanthropic activities, and wrote and performed music.

After completion of this series she was given a series of radiotherapy treatments because of an unidentified mass in her upper thorax. She lost her voice, was hospitalized because of a pleural effusion, and died in hospital while undergoing a second series of chemotherapy sessions. I visited her in hospital, reinforced her ability to breathe relatively comfortably and to withdraw into a trance-sleep whenever she felt too tired to maintain contact with her family, during their frequent visits. She suffered more nausea than with her first series, but it was controlled with medication and self-hypnosis.

Following her death, her daughter told me that her mother had been calmer and more content with her life during her last year than ever before. This daughter attributed her mother's mental peace to her psychotherapy.

Summary

There are several elements that form the basis of treating the side effects of chemotherapy in cancer patients:

1. Treatment of the whole patient, with emphasis on building hope. The hope may be invested in survival and resumption of life, or, in some terminal cases, may be attached to an expectation of prolongation of life, in relative comfort.
2. Management of unnecessary fear and pain are, of course, important. Fear, pain and nausea are interdependent.
3. Disruption of the pattern of symptoms, including pain and nausea. Sensory modalities can be modified.
4. Time sequences can be changed and time distortion may be utilized to alter patterns. A person can go through an entire response in a short time, perhaps minutes instead of hours.
5. All of the above can be connected with sleep or drowsiness, especially in patients who do not have to be active.
6. In lieu of sleepiness, a clear-minded meditative state may be induced, sometimes associated with "mystical" feelings or psychedelic experiences.
7. Sense of appetite can be enhanced. Suggestions of hunger can be followed by suggestions of sleep, especially before the patient has time to experience nausea or vomiting.

When everything else fails, the induction of a deep sleep can often be accomplished by means of hypnosis. This type of escape can be very helpful, not only from the torments of pain, fear and despair, but also from feelings of nausea and dizziness which may accompany the chemotherapy.

Afterword

Working and living with cancer patients often evoke symptoms in treating personnel—mostly through the process of sympathetic identification. Physicians and nurses will develop pains and weakness, associated with hidden and sometimes not so hidden convictions that they have acquired cancer themselves. They also can become nauseated and feel febrile while dealing with the side effects of chemotherapy in their patients.

Psychotherapists or hypnotherapists who are working in these situations can develop similar responses. Obviously, we have tools—the ones I have outlined in this chapter—to deal with this kind of response. In fact, in alleviating our own nausea, our own pains, our own fears, we can develop a wider range of approaches to help our patients. We can explore different types of imagery, different types of relaxation suggestions, diversion suggestions and ways of evoking hopeful feelings in ourselves. By a combination of introspection, self-hypnosis and action we can reach a balanced perspective. Erickson once told me that he was able to maintain a type of separation from patients because, as he said, "I know my own voice." With the help of the techniques I have outlined we can find an optimal degree of joining and separation with our patients and can learn from and with them.

Note

1 This chapter was previously published in *Ericksonian Psychotherapy II: Clinical Applications*, edited by Jeffrey Zeig, 1985 as Chapter 28, pp. 387–398.

References

Erickson, M.H. (1980). Migraine Headache in a Resistant Patient. In E.L. Rossi (ed.), *The Collected Papers of Milton H. Erickson, Vol. 4: Innovative Hypnotherapy* (pp. 252–254). New York: Irvington.
Hall, H.R. (1982). Hypnosis and the Immune System: A Review with Implications for Cancer and the Psychology of Healing. *American Journal of Clinical Hypnosis*, 25(2–3): 92–103.
Morrow, G.R., and Morrell, C. (1982). Behavioral Treatment for the Anticipatory Nausea and Vomiting Induced By Cancer Chemotherapy. *The New England Journal of Medicine*, 307(24): 1476–1480.
Newton, B.W. (1982). The Use of Hypnosis in the Treatment of Cancer Patients. *American Journal of Clinical Hypnosis*, 25(2–3): 104–113.
Redd, W.H., Rosenberger, P.H., and Hendler, C.S. (1982–1983). Controlling Chemotherapy Side Effects. *American Journal of Clinical Hypnosis*, 25(2–3): 161–172.
Simonton, O.C., Simonton, S., and Creighton, J.L. (1978). *Getting Well Again*. Los Angeles: Tarcher.

7

A GUIDED FANTASY[1]

Introduction

This chapter presents the transcript of a group hypnotic induction, with 30 people in the audience. In "A Guided Fantasy," I guided the group into a trance, and gave them the opportunity to experience some of their own unconscious learnings, ones that they may have consciously forgotten about. I used the memorable image of walking down a marble staircase onto a beach, to deepen their trance, and to prepare them for this suggestion: as an adult, you can go back and find yourself as a young child. I'm suggesting that you can go into a trance and bring back whatever is of value to you. It's another way of suggesting that many things are in your unconscious mind, but you don't know they're there. In hypnosis you can tap into those unconscious learnings and utilize them.

Essentially, the goal of my hypnotic suggestions is to help people tap into this thing we call the unconscious mind. Once they can do this, they can go into a trance initially and they can emerge from the trance, bringing back with them whatever has been useful, whatever they've tapped into. All of your past learnings and experiences are stored in the unconscious and in the trance state, you can access your past learnings and experiences.

This chapter includes some of my favorite inductions, like the early learning set induction. The therapist asks, "Do you know the difference between the letter B and the letter D, or the letter A and the letter O?" Those are early things we learn, reminding people of things they learned when they're very young, things they go back to automatically.

Poetry is an important part of hypnotic induction and so many of the inductions that Erickson used and that I used are poetic. The choice of words, the rhythm, the meter, the rhymes – all those are poetic. If you go through the words verbatim, other things in my induction could be called poetic. The language is important. Instead of just saying prosaically that "everything you've learned to do is stored somehow in your mind, in what we call unconscious learnings," I'm saying it in a more poetic way, repeating everything, everything, everything over and over again. This poetic imagery came to me as I was channeling my unconscious. It came from my associations as I remembered things that Erickson had said at different times.

The idea of going over a mountain I used from Erickson, who had used that image when he hypnotized me once. But other images are my own, such as going down the marble steps. Those are things that came to me. The image of going down the marble steps can help the person get in touch with his or her inner self, concretized as marble.

It's possible to give much shorter inductions. I was guided in what to say by my own free associations and allowed myself to go into a trance. I then guided people to find their own images and their own feelings as they went into themselves. It's not necessary to have such an elaborate, time consuming induction but for a large group, providing many different approaches allowed each person to find his or her own "hypnotic experience."

Freud saw the unconscious as being made up of ego and id; those are impulses that were more primitive, more basic, than our conscious organized thoughts. Freud tended to emphasize the unacceptable thoughts and feelings which go into the unconscious and Freudian therapy initially consisted of changing unconscious processes to conscious ones, available to the conscious mind.

Erickson's view of the unconscious is not just that negative, unacceptable things are put there because they couldn't be accepted or dealt with. He included positive as well as negative memories in the unconscious. His unconscious was much more akin to Jung's vision of the "collective unconscious", which includes things we learn because we're part of a group. The whole group has reactions and responses, and he called it the collective unconscious. Jung also saw positive potential ideas and impulses as being part of a person's unconscious. Freud's unconscious is based primarily on the past. Jung's unconscious is sometimes called a teleological approach, because it's based on possibilities for the future, possibilities of making new learnings, taking from the unknown future and finding new images that create new learning. Erickson's unconscious included new learnings, so it's closer to Jung than to Freud.

How did Erickson believe that we could find what I call new learnings? In a dream for example, we may find solutions to problems based on trying out new possibilities. That's why I encouraged people to have their past selves accompany their future selves to the present, so they could access these new learnings.

I always tried to use new images in different inductions. In this group induction I used new images to evoke deep experiences from several people, and individual ones from each person.

The images are always based on what I'm working on, on that individual's tendencies. Also, I try to recognize and tap into a person's particular way of imagining. Some people are more tactile, some people are more visual, some people are more auditory. The images I present for them as possibilities will include many of these sensations.

***

The Induction

So, I would like to tell you all how excited I am at the opportunity to be with you and to guide you in this trance that we will enjoy together today. It's very rare that I get a full hour just to allow myself to enjoy a trance. And I don't know what this experience is going to be like for me. I'm sure you don't know what it's going to be like for you either. The only thing that I'm certain is that it will be interesting, maybe some surprises. As Erickson always said: every child likes a surprise. I'm sure that you all have different—well, what they call minor agendas—things that you would like to explore: things that you would like to see, if you could-experience, that you have not experienced before in other trances or without trance. And I'm also sure that most of you at least will experience much more than you hope for. To give you a chance to orient yourself: we know, where we are now, don't we? We are in Phoenix, Arizona, in the Falstaff room at the Civic Center. The time is two minutes after eleven. We started very promptly. I'm used to working by the hour, I don't know whether most of you are or not. I'm going to make this into a ... well ... perhaps we'll make it into about a 50-minute hour, so we'll have ten minutes just to reorient ourselves at the end, afterwards. And we'll reorient ourselves at that time to be back here in Phoenix in the Flagstaff room at the Civic Center at exactly 11:50 A.M. Phoenix time.

The first thing I would like to tell you about my way of working with trance is that in a hypnotic trance you don't have to do anything. You don't have to move, you don't have to talk, you don't have to listen consciously to my words. I understand that when a person comes into this room or any other room, he or she brings with him or her a conscious mind and an unconscious mind. Now the conscious mind is interested, is observing, is curious, perhaps it's doubting, questioning, wondering, examining: those are the jobs of the conscious mind. Now your unconscious mind can be thought of as a vast reservoir of learnings, as Erickson described it, as everything that you have ever experienced, everything that you have ever done, everything that you have ever heard, everything that you have ever learned, everything that you have ever tasted or smelled or hoped for is stored somewhere, and most of it is stored in the part of the mind that we think of as the unconscious mind. And in your trance you can get in touch with some of those unconscious learnings, you can find some that will be very useful for you, that will help you to move in directions that are really constructive for you, will help you to explore areas that are either undeveloped, or just ready to become developed. And you can use those unconscious learnings for purposes that you may be barely aware of and for other purposes that you only become aware of after you have used them. So, we are sitting here in Phoenix, in the Flagstaff room, our eyes are open, mostly: some are closed. If your eyes are open, you begin to notice changes in the way the air looks. Somewhat warped perhaps, things get smaller and larger, you hear Dr. Rosen's voice coming sometimes from very close, at other times from very far away. You feel sensations in your body. Some of them are unpleasant sensations—feelings of tension, feelings of anxiety, feelings of tightness, and others are very pleasant—a tingling feeling here and there, energy flowing from the top of your head to the bottom of your feet. If you want to have a Kundalini-type experience, you could have that. Or a Kabbalistic-type experience, where you focus on Kefer, the spot just above your head. I want you to do that: you could visualize the bright light just above your head. And from that bright light source of energy is a flowing, sweet wave, flowing down over your face, down over your shoulders, your chest and your back, your abdomen-and to the pelvic area: down your sides, legs, drawing out any of that tension, any of that anxiety, any of those pains that were there before, like a warmth, only it's moving, like immersing yourself in a healing lotion, isn't it? And it feels so good, does it not? And you can become now, if you like, a bodiless mind. And the bodiless mind can travel anywhere in time or in space. You can go back and find that young person that you were, beginning to learn so many things, learning to read and to write. And just to tell the difference between the letter "a" and the letter "o," is a difficult task. And how do you put together a straight line and a little circle to make a "b" or a "d" or a "q" or a "p?" And are there two bumps on the "n" and three on the "m" or are there two bumps on the "m" and three on the "n"? And do you dot the "t" and cross the "i" or do you dot the "i" and cross the "t"? And what makes it even more difficult: is that there are small letters and capital letters, there are written letters and there are printed letters. And you learned to form all of those letters. You learned to write them ... automatically. When you grow up, you will not have to think about each letter any more. You write things automatically. And there are still things to write even when you are all grown up. And you could enjoy writing them in your own way, your own style, more and more automatically as you learn to trust your own unconscious mind, because that little child grows older, minute by minute, hour by hour, day by day, week by week, month by month, year by year, until one day he or she knows who she is, who he is.

Now in my way of living I sometimes like to climb a mountain and I always wonder, what's on the other side? I know that on my side of the mountain there are buildings, there are paved streets, there are fields, there are lights, there are trees and rocks and a lot of people. But on the other side of the mountain there could be a desert ... dark and foreboding. And I always *know* that, no matter how foreboding that desert is, I'll find something there of value, of interest for me. Sometimes I may be afraid of what I'll see on the other side. I always *know*, that I can climb to the top and take a quick peek over to the other side. And if I don't like what I see, I can always return to my side of the mountain. [Pause]

Putting it another way—you can walk down the street and reach a corner. You may decide that you want to turn that corner. But you are not certain whether you want to continue in the new direction that you have chosen. And you can always take a quick look around the corner and see whether or not you like what is there. If you don't like it, you can always continue in the direction in which you were going.

And to balance the city life I find it's very helpful for me to go to the country and enjoy nature. If you would like to join me on a walk through the woods you can do that. Or while I'm walking through the woods you might want to walk along the beach. Find your own place, your own special favorite environment. When I'm walking through my woods, I sometimes feel as if I'm entering into a cathedral, the branches of the pine trees covering the entrance of the path into the woods, into the cathedral. You can smell the pine aroma, a very fresh clean aroma, isn't it? In the south of France, they feel that it's very good for your lungs, when you walk into the woods, you can feel the carpet of pine needles on the ground, very soft, spongy and springy and supportive. As I go deeper and deeper into the woods, step by step—one at a time, I know that I can stop at whatever spot I wish. I can always leave the woods when I want. I'm drawn by my curiosity to go in still deeper and see some colorful mushrooms over there, blue mushrooms? They really are blue. And red ones, yellow with red spots on them. There are tall mushrooms and there are some that are just spread out along the wood of a dead tree. And the leaves are still present on the trees, and you can hear them rustling with the wind, if you listen carefully.

I remember, when I was very small, I would have climbed on one of those trees. It seemed so high up. I knew that even if I fell down, the ground is very soft. You can climb as high as you want. No bird flies too high as long as it flies with its own wings. And as we continue still deeper into the woods, we may run into an orchard, it's a magic orchard actually, as there are trees that have golden apples, silver plums, rubies, sapphires, diamonds. So we know that we are in a magic world now, a world of childhood. And in this magic world we can get any help that we need. We can call upon a healing fairy, if we need healing. And there she is! We can call upon a wise old woman to tell us what we should do; what shall we do about that decision that we have to make. That's right! She has an answer. Or we can just decide to play and to enjoy being here in special ways as time stops. And we have all the time that we need in the time that is available to accomplish what you really want to accomplish. We can become clear about what it is that we really want to accomplish, push away all that confusing bush, all those weeds. You can see very clearly now where the true growth lies. It doesn't always lie, sometimes it tells the truth, reaching up to all the sky, embracing the clouds. And we can go out as far out as we want beyond the clouds to the planets. Or we can stay securely here, protected, warm, enjoying a cool breath on our forehead. And we take a large breath and breathe out, and in and out, and out and back, all in the rhythms of the days and the nights, the sun and the moon, and really enjoy this exploring and resting, contracting and expanding with every breath.

You can always return to your friend or guide—in the woods or on the seashore or wherever you want.

And who would like to take another trip with me? If you have rested from this one, please nod your head when you are ready to start. This trip will be especially useful for those of you who are interested in stopping smoking. Those of you who want to continue the trip you are already on, just do so; you don't have to go with us now. Follow your own path, your own agenda and enjoy your trip. Maybe you'll tell us about it sometime in the future, when we come together again.

I'm going now to remind you of an experience that you had many, many times in your childhood. You are sleeping in your own bed and you are having a dream. And in your dream, you get out of bed and you go into a closet over there. In the back of the closet is a door. When you look for that door, tomorrow morning, when you wake up, you will not find it there. But it's there now. And the door opens very easily, and you walk through the door, and you are on the top of a very old interesting stairway, maybe a marble stairway, because the stone is very, very smooth, and you can even feel the polished marble of the bannister under one of your hands. You go downstairs, step by step, really enjoying the feeling of support from that firm stone. You may want to kick off your shoes, when you are part way down, so that you can feel the smoothness and the coolness of the marble underneath your feet. It does feel good, doesn't it? You go deeper and deeper with every step that you take. Just like that. Now at the bottom of the stairs you walk out onto a beach. The sand is very silky smooth, fine sand, you can feel that under your feet now, can't you? [Pause] You step out onto the beach. As you walk along the beach, you see the ocean over to the side, and the surf is coming in and going out, coming in and out—in and out—in and out with your breathing. And as you look out over that vast expanse of ocean in front of you, you may be aware of the fact, that the salt concentration in that water is exactly the same as in your own bloodstream. You can appreciate the fact, as you enjoy the beauty and the immensity of the power of this ocean, that you are a part of this world of beauty, of nature. Your body is a part of this natural world—the world of nature. And you are beautiful, and your body is also beautiful. [Pause] You walk along the beach, step by step; you reach a large stone standing in the middle of the beach. It's very rough in some places, and in other places it's very polished, like the marble on that staircase, polished by thousands and thousands and thousands of years of water. And really, it's interesting, isn't it? —to feel the difference between the rough parts and the smooth parts. We can think of what Milton Erickson said about roughage, that sickness and pain and troubles are the roughage of life. And if anybody has ever eaten Army food—that spam that processed food—he realizes how important roughage is in one's diet.

You can get a firm hold on some of the smooth parts too, and that feels so good, doesn't it? And you look into a hole in the rock there, a deep deep hole, very very tiny, not big enough to put your hand into. At the bottom of the hole is a very precious jewel. You may wonder, how you can get that jewel for yourself, if you really want it. It is very valuable. It would give you a lot of the things that you really want in this life. You don't have to get it right now. And think about it, as you walk farther along the beach. And you can always return to this rock also, as you can return to any of the places that you have visited on this trip today. You easily can go back to anyone of them at any time, just by closing your eyes, as they are closed now and picturing that particular place. You have been there, and once you have been here, you can always come back—at your own time and in your own way, to either where you experienced something that you started to experience here today or to have a new experience. So you walk along the beach, come to a garden. The garden has the most beautiful flowers that you have ever seen. Some of them are very large and very colorful—like jungle flowers, but there is a very, very fine, very delicate petal, that is floating over there on the surface of the pond—so delicate and so fine. The only thing you can compare it with would be the very delicate membranes in your own body. It's as delicate as the alveoli in your lungs, the place where oxygen moves through as it goes from the air into your bloodstream. You realize that the tissues and the membranes in your own body are even more delicate than that delicate flower petal. And those flowers are really beautiful, aren't they? Very favorite colors and scents. And you realize, that they are beautiful, because they get plenty of nourishment, get clean air, and they are protected from the winds, when they become too rough, and yet they are invigorated and strengthened by some wind, by some changes in climate. And wouldn't we do everything to protect a beautiful flower, if we could help it? Wouldn't we? We would do everything to help such beautiful living creatures. [Pause] So as we are enjoying colors, the aromas, sensations, the breathing freely of this clean air, you walk back along the beach, return to our staircase. You walk up step by step, begin feeling the friendliness and the support of those steps.

Climbing step by step back to that room, where you were lying and dreaming, dreaming that we took that whole walk through the doorway at the back of the closet, down the stairs, along the beach, into the garden and back again. At the same time, you, as an adult can go back and find that young child, the child who may be really suffering, who may be having a good time, but more likely having some real problems, feeling all alone, even in dreams, feeling a lot of pain, feeling that no one understands the child. You can tell the child that you do understand it, you may want to hug the child, tell the child that things will work out, if you want, you can take the child by the hand and lead the child into its future. It's your present, and she will know, he will know, that he will never be alone again. The child can begin to awaken from a dream, and you as an adult can begin to awaken from your trance in your own time and in your own way. Bring back with you whatever is of value for you and leave the rest behind to develop, to be revisited, reexamined at some later time. And don't come out of your trance too quickly! You have plenty of time, and if you would like to experience something really interesting, I suggest doing something that is not easy, but it's not too difficult either. You could awaken from your trance just from the neck up at first and feel the difference between your head and the rest of your body. If you want to do that with your eyes open, just move your head, but not the rest of your body. I think you'll find a very interesting difference. And as you wake up, you feel wider and wider awake. You can feel as if you had a really good rest: You return from a long, restful, healing, refreshing vacation. And that feeling can remain with you for the rest of this conference. And you will enjoy the rest of this conference. I'm sure I will, because I always enjoy learning new things. And I've enjoyed this trip we have taken together with you today.

It's almost 11:50, and we are here in the Flagstaff room, the Civic Center, Phoenix, Arizona, December 5, 1986. Hi!

If there is anybody who has any trouble getting back, please come up and talk with me. And I hope, you get back to wherever you want to be. But I think, from what I can see, that most of you are quite happy with where you are right now ... aren't you?

No? Yes? Not sure yet? You will have to give yourself a chance to get oriented. See what you are left with and what you want to take with you. O.K. [Pause] It will take you a few minutes to fully go back to your usual state of consciousness, if you want to go back there. But enjoy wherever you are. You'll feel different when you start moving around than you do now, probably.

Any questions or any comments? Not everybody is ready to move. Some people are moving, that's fine. You leave it to whenever you are ready to. If anybody wants to make any comments, any questions, that might be of interest to the rest, you can do that. If you want to talk to me individually, come up and talk to me. O.K.

Comments

Sidney Rosen's guided trance is an inward journey, starting in the Flagstaff room of the Civic Center in Phoenix, Arizona, the actual location, and ending there 50 minutes later. It shows how the conditions of time and space can be utilized as a frame for trance work. Having paced the situation and assisted dissociation of the conscious and the unconscious, he leads us inwards by helping us to focus on visual, auditory and kinesthetic perceptions. I guess this sequence is deliberate, with Sidney Rosen bringing in his spiritual knowledge and helping us to become a bodiless mind very quickly. After taking us back to an early learning state, he invites us to join him mountain climbing and then wondering, "what's on the other side" of the mountain or reaching a corner and being told "turn that corner." To deepen the trance, he invites us to accompany him "deeper and deeper into the woods." This induction is a clear example of how the symbolism of nature can be utilized for the process, in which we finally find ourselves in the magic world of childhood, in a magic orchard, where we can get every form of help. With the orchard theme is seeded the final goal, the lovely garden, where we shall be at the deepest point of this trance. At this stage there is a confusing interruption, the possibility of coming back, with Sidney Rosen using the technique of a fractionated trance in the form of an invitation to come out of trance and find security by checking if everything is all right in order to go much deeper afterwards. This also serves as a check for the therapist, because he can now obtain a clear response from the audience and find out if the people are still in contact with him.

The new journey down into an even deeper trance picks up the theme of childhood and starts descending into the dreamworld, step by step down a marble stairway, another familiar, traditional symbol. Finally, we face the ocean of the unconscious on our walk along the beach, see the jewel in the hole in the rock, a symbol for a point we can't even reach, and find the lovely garden.

I remember from my experience that I became creative at this point, sucked the jewel out of the rock with my mouth and felt very contented because of this idea.

An especially moving and healing experience within this trance is Sidney Rosen's careful leading back to the present, the return part so often ignored, almost neglected or sadly shortened during trance inductions. Why miss these opportunities! At the very end Sidney Rosen invites people to talk to him individually also. This, too, is something I have often missed in many other group inductions with strange people. I really appreciate Sidney Rosen's offer, I think everybody who does a group induction with people one doesn't know should express this invitation, if possible.

Note

1 This chapter was previously published in *Ericksonian Hypnotherapeutic Group Inductions*, 1991, edited by Hildegard and Klippstein, as Chapter 18, pp. 129–135.

8

RECENT EXPERIENCES WITH GESTALT, ENCOUNTER AND HYPNOTIC TECHNIQUES[1]

Introduction

I first met Milton Erickson in 1970. Our first meeting reinforced my feelings about the importance of experiencing the past in the present. I had vague memories of traveling from Detroit, where I was born in 1926, to London, Ontario, where my family moved when I was five years old. But when I accessed those memories with Erickson, I felt the same feelings of anxiety and apprehension that I had experienced at the time. I felt as if I was not just remembering the experience but having it at that moment. In that sense, I wasn't re-experiencing the journey, but simply experiencing it.

Once a patient accesses an experience, along with the physical sensations that go with it—including heat, shaking, or heart palpitations—the therapist can introduce corrective experiences, such as the sensation of being relaxed rather than anxious during the journey. The result of my first meeting with Erickson changed my approach and led to different techniques for evoking experiences from the past, not simply as memories but as re-experiences. At the end of 1970, months after meeting Erickson, I published some of those reflections in this article in the *American Journal of Psychoanalysis*, "Recent Experiences with Encounter, Gestalt, and Hypnotic Techniques."

The techniques discussed in this chapter can be applied and experienced with or without a formal hypnotic induction, individually or in groups. My experience with Gestalt and Encounter techniques, however, is that going into a trance in a group can be very helpful, because a notional response can be experienced as more real with group support. Expressing emotions in the present tense in front of an expectant audience, people can wipe out the distinction between a perceived or imagined experience and a real one, happening in the here and now. If a patient has to say her name in front of a group, it's different than saying it alone; some patients actually faint. Interventions in a group setting, such as pounding on pillows or grasping the therapist's arm, can be so powerful that, in some cases, it's not necessary to add a hypnotic induction. The experiences themselves allow the possibility that a person can experience the squeezing of the therapist's arm as if she was actually choking her father.

Experiencing a memory feels real more than just remembering, or intellectualizing, or talking: the actual experiencing of the choking bypasses the intellectual process. Therapeutic techniques such as time regression ("you are three years old") can help patients experience the past as if it is happening right now. Therapists can also use gestalt techniques, including concrete attention to detail, doing instead of talking, and accepting responsibility for one's own behavior.

The goal of all these techniques isn't just for patients to relive experiences; we want them to have corrective experiences. For example, when a patient talks about his experience with his father while choking the therapist's arm, his feelings are not experienced as a detached memory and therefore he can assume responsibility for his feelings. Later, he can switch positions and play the top dog rather than the underdog. Rather than simply manipulating the role in his mind, he can actually experience it and correct it. Recalling a memory is one thing. But by looking at a memory differently than when we first had an experience, we can recall things we've learned in the meantime, and incorporate that unconscious learning into our corrected experience.

***

Health—Or Flight into Health

I had been treating a 35-year-old professor for about two years. Among his most disturbing concerns were his compulsion to visit restrooms and his inability to complete the manuscripts required for his professional advancement. For one year he had been attending group therapy sessions once a week in addition to individual psychotherapy sessions every second week.

The incident described here occurred during his 40th group session which took place immediately following one of his individual analytic hours.

During the latter hour, the patient was hypnotized, for perhaps the thirtieth time. Under hypnosis he regressed to a level where, at first, he indicated that he could not talk and, finally, with much sobbing and gasping, expressed, very dramatically, his feeling that he had killed his mother being born. Feeling that he was on the verge of some sort of "breakthrough" a post-hypnotic suggestion was made that, during the very next group session, he would express very essential feelings which would lead to some crucial insights for him.

During his year of group therapy, he had generally remained a silent observer or had limited himself to detached, intellectualized comments on the behavior of others. On this day he was, typically, silent for forty-five minutes, and appeared to be occupied with his own thoughts. When he made a comment about the behavior of one of the young women in the group, I took the opportunity to challenge him to stand up, walk across the room and express his feelings towards this woman. He insisted that he could not even stand up. The group then spent 20 minutes urging, challenging and encouraging him to try. He seemed to shrink further and further into his seat. Then, when attention to him was momentarily diverted, he quickly got up, made a half-hearted show of hugging the girl and then sat in silence for another twenty minutes. Finally, while someone else was talking, he suddenly interjected with five minutes remaining in the session: "That's what I always do! I always wait until it is too late and then I get involved in things!"

Since he had always refused to try any type of physical encounter, he was then challenged to engage in a pushing contest with another group member, ostensibly to prove that he had changed. He accepted the challenge, with only mild reluctance this time. He was showing considerable strength when he suddenly complained of a pain in his right shoulder muscle. I massaged the shoulder while giving him strong suggestions of relaxation and the pain disappeared within one minute. He continued the pushing and left the group session feeling very tired and elated.

Two weeks later he announced to the group that he was working well at his writing, that he was developing a wholesome interest in a girl he had been dating for two months. He stated that he had decided that he would like to try working out his own situations without therapy. He terminated therapy that evening, with the approval of three quarters of the people in the group and with my somewhat cautious approval as well. Eight months later he returned to meet the group members after a session, without prior notice and without consulting me. He wanted to tell them that he was getting married in two weeks, that he was publishing a great deal and that he wanted to thank them for the important role they had played in his life.

When this story is related to some analysts, their first response is: "He probably dropped out of therapy, made a flight into health perhaps to avoid entering into a panic after you massaged his neck." Or they will attribute some other unwholesome motives to him. Perhaps it is a sign of our own lack of belief in the possibilities of growth and our over-commitment to a skeptical, "scientific" approach that when we are presented with apparent improvement—a patient feels and acts cured of a serious difficulty—our first professional and emotional response tends to be "how is the patient fooling himself and us?" Yet for the purposes of this discussion the focus is primarily on the fact that this patient changed dramatically after an apparently crucial session, that he was moved to some new activities and attitudinal changes and that these changes were sustained and subsequently led to further change. What were the pertinent factors which most contributed to the changes—are these factors seen in other forms of therapeutic intervention? Can they be used in a more organized fashion and with greater awareness than previously employed?

Some Innovative Hypnotic Techniques

In the case history just outlined, the roles of suggestion or hypnosis are apparently significant. Additional concepts about hypnosis will be discussed later. The assigning of physical tasks to the patient was one of my first entrees into the area of what has become popularized as encounter therapy. For several years, though, I had been less concerned about the well-known dangers of assuming a more active role in working with patients and more concerned about those patients who seemed to continue on and on in so-called therapy with very little changing, growing, self-realizing.

In exploring other techniques to supplement the relatively non-directive ones of psychoanalysis, I had re-discovered my old interest in hypnosis had applied hypnosis as so-called hypnoanalysis and had experimented with many of the imaginative techniques and approaches which ingenious therapeutic innovators such as Milton Erickson (Haley, 1967) and Leuner have described. I had found, with some patients, that "sensory hypnoplasty" (Raginsky, 1962) helped. This is the fantasy stimulating technique in which a person, hypnotized or not, is given a piece of softened colored plasticine, often mixed with strong cheese or other odiferous substances. The patient is encouraged to "do with the clay whatever you like, let yourself go as completely as possible." Often this approach results in intense emotional abreaction. In my hands, though, it did not help sufficiently to warrant the cumbersome preparations of the materials that was necessary. Sacerdote's technique of "Hallucinated Sensory Hypnoplasty," in which the person is hypnotized and given suggestions that he can see and feel the clay was just as helpful, much less messy and less time-consuming.

I found myself searching, as I'm sure some jaded therapists are searching, for other effective ways of evoking emotional responses in intellectualized patients, for ways of helping obsessive, alienated patients to have experiences with other ways of thinking, feeling and acting.

Leuner's "guided fantasies" and Sacerdote's "guided hypnotic dreams" (Sacerdote, 1967, p. 205) provided refreshingly new experiences for some. Other patients responded well to hypnotic age regression while still others were able to get in touch with deep and meaningful feelings simply by being instructed to "feel your feelings" or to "let your feelings build up." These effects could be obtained with or without a formal hypnotic induction.

Recent Experiments on the Nature of Hypnosis

In the course of working with hypnosis again I discovered what experimenters such as T.X. Barber (Barber, 1967) and Martin Orne (Orne, 1967) have described in comparatively recent work with hypnosis. They have found:

1. That it is impossible to find any *objective* criteria for deciding when a person is hypnotized and that,

2. So far as some of their subjects' ability to respond to suggestions was concerned, *it made no apparent difference whether or not they underwent any type of formal hypnotic induction.*

For example, in their experiments, control subjects tolerate as much, or more pain, as "hypnotized" ones. Some patients demonstrate more strength in the "waking" state than in the "hypnotized" one. Barber has used his findings to question the validity of the entire concept of hypnosis and writes the word in quotations. Others, more in sympathy with the hypnotic pioneer Milton Erickson, feel that there is a phenomenon which has traditionally been called a hypnotic "trance", that this is a unique state of awareness and receptivity to hetero and auto-suggestions and that, when in this state, a person can focus attention and have his attention directed by the hypnotist into uniquely vivid and subjectively "real" forms of experiencing of memories, of present perceptions and, often, of objects suggested by the hypnotist. I tend to favor Erickson's views—recognizing that the experimental work of Barber and Orne showed that *effects previously thought attainable only after a hypnotic induction could be obtained without such an induction in some people.* Recent work on "autonomic conditioning" by Kamlya (Kamlya, 1969) and others in which subjects, without hypnotic induction, learn to control their own brainwaves, blood pressure, or hand temperature, indicate that concepts such as motivation, reinforcement and Orne's "demand characteristics of the situation" (Orne, 1967) are more significant in determining a person's behavior, autonomic as well as voluntary, than whether or not he follows the criteria for deep hypnosis on a scale for hypnotic susceptibility. If "imagining" a state of health can clear up a skin rash or plantar warts, let's learn how to develop and intensify this imagining power. We may call the procedure "hypnosis" or not according to our taste.

"Presentness"—A Link Between, Horney and Existentialism

One of the best ways of evoking and intensifying vivid feelings and images is that which was developed largely in work with hypnotic age regression and hypnotic "time progression". This is to ask the patient to describe events and perceptions in the *present* tense—with directions such as "It is happening *right now.*" "You *are* three years old (or 90 years old). You feel and think and act at that age."

Fritz Perls, in devising techniques that he calls "gimmicks" in his "Gestalt Therapy", has carried this knowledge of the importance of "presentness" from his earlier work with hypnosis. Perhaps he was also influenced by his working in supervision with Karen Horney in Berlin. In any case, he not only emphasizes the "Here and Now, the What and How," as Horney did, but insists that all memories of the past and plans for the future, dreams, fantasies, be expressed in the present tense, preferably acted, with the patient playing all the roles, one at a time.

Gestalt Therapy—Principles and Examples

What are some of the Gestalt Therapy principles? In addition to its present-centeredness (Naranjo, 1967) the most important of these principles may be listed under three headings as was done by Enright (Enright, 1967). These are:

1. Concrete attention to detail rather than abstract conceptualizing (Perls calls abstracting and intellectualizing "intellectual garbage" or even "elephant-shit").
2. Doing, with organismic involvement, instead of talking *about*.
3. Accepting responsibility for one's own behavior instead of denying, projecting, attributing, displacing, etc.

In order to help actualize these principles Perls has devised several techniques which he frankly calls "gimmicks" (Perls, 1969).

In group workshops one of these gimmicks is his "hot seat" approach. In this, the patient is always guided towards experiencing himself where *he* is first. If hostility is then expressed or he is urged to touch someone, it is done only after he is very much aware of his isolation, alienation, etc.

The patient, for example, volunteers to sit in the "hot seat." He may say "I don't know what I want to work on." Or "I want to talk about a dream." Whatever his introduction, he is directed to focus on where he *is* at the moment. This is done with questions such as: "What are you feeling at this moment?" "Where are you experiencing your nervousness?" "How?" If he says: "I can't think of anything," It is suggested that he rephrase this as "I am blocking my thinking or my feeling." He is then asked to describe precisely how he is experiencing both the block and the blocking tendencies. If, when he is asked about his nervousness, he says that he cannot feel anything, he is asked specifically "What do you feel in your taste? Your chest, your hands? Your testicles?" If he says that he feels a shakiness in his fingers he is asked to show this—to shake his fingers, even to exaggerate the shaking until he can feel both his responsibility for shaking them and his concomitant emotions, thoughts and fantasies. If he feels and expresses anger this is done only after the above process is experienced. The anger is not dissociated from him. In fact, it is very much *connected* with him, He may then be asked "Whom do you see (in your mind) when you feel this anger?" Often, he will respond with "my father" or "my mother," Only then is he urged to act out a dialogue with his father. He may pound on a pillow or choke the therapist's arm or use whatever mode best intensifies and expresses his actual feeling at that moment. This approach is a far cry from a thoughtless, mechanical, manufactured or non-directed encouragement of hostility expression as encouraged by some untrained "trainers." At all times the feelings expressed are connected with the patient—with his present and his past. The therapist insists that the patient assume responsibility for *his* feelings, *his* words and *his* actions.

Later more complex and more conflicted feelings are expressed—often with the patient changing chairs or assuming different postures in order to more clearly experience them. In the classical "top dog"—"underdog" inner dialogue, for example, the patient will be instructed to sit in a higher chair when expressing the top dog part in himself—the voice that says such things as "You should" "Who do you think you are?" "You've never been any good"—the demanding, critical, judging voice—Freud's superego, Horney's "shoulds", Berne's "parent." He changes to a stool when expressing the "underdog"—the criticized part, the child, the meek part, the hopeless part. Generally, he "writes his own dialogue," but if he has difficulty at times the therapist may suggest "lines." For example, let us assume that the patient is intellectualizing while playing "top dog." He is intellectually talking about the fact that he cannot accept his indecisiveness. The therapist may suggest, "Let me feed you a line—try saying to meek little indecisive John 'I hate you.'" Patient may venture cautiously starting in a matter-of-fact voice to say the words. He is asked to repeat them—louder and louder—until therapist, patient and group are convinced that this is a *genuine* feeling and that the patient owns it as his own. It may have been brought out by borrowed words but if it does not fit it must be discarded. And matters are not *left* here. The patient is not dismissed with only the satisfaction of being able to clearly express an honest, strong feeling—although, for many, this alone is no small accomplishment. He is asked to feel and then to describe the feelings of being the "top dog" hater. He then is asked to sit in the "underdog" stool in order to get in touch with that part too. He is encouraged to go back and forth—in each case being asked "Did you hear your voice?" After going to the other chair he is asked "What is your response?" After a few shifts he often will say: "I'm confused, which am I now? Top dog or underdog?" By this time the voices in both chairs begin to sound almost alike. He may feel himself stuck at what Perls calls an "impasse." He may be dismissed then to resolve the impasse in his own time and place or he may be encouraged to continue the inner dialogue right there, trying different attitudes in both positions. For example, if, as top dog, he has been using his father as a model, speaking in his father's voice and telling himself, as underdog, "You're no good and never will be" he may be asked at the point of impasse to have his father, as top dog, try the line "I really love you, my son." If he can say this sincerely to his underdog, to himself, and this is by no means easy, it means that he has already undergone some shift in his self-acceptance. Saying the words, without conviction is useless. I find that even a good actor cannot do this convincingly if he does not feel it applying to himself. The therapist and group are very good judges of the genuineness or phoniness of his emotions although the patient is generally asked "Did you really mean that?" or "Do you take responsibility for holding on to your anger?" or "Did that sound genuine to you?"

Taking Back Externalizations

We know the importance of taking back our externalizations (Perls calls them projections). But how to do this? Perls has his subjects act them out—"be them." His theoretical basis for this is similar to that of Horney, i.e., that the characteristics in others which disturb us, or upon which we are focused, are often those which we are denying in ourselves and externalizing to them. To "complete our Gestalt" we must not only intellectually be able to say "yes, I am really selfish, cruel, vain or what have you," but we must be able to feel this and own it. For example, when Joan, a young physician, spent hour after hour railing against her mother for the latter's vanity, selfishness, frivolousness, and lack of respect for her, I could have talked in Horney's terms about her claims on mother, the hurts to her pride from mother's neglect, lack of appreciation or criticisms of her. Instead, I suggested to her "Be your mother, say for me, *I* am vain, selfish and frivolous." She said it, without much conviction. I had her repeat it and she then admitted that she really was vain, selfish, and frivolous. Characteristically, she quickly followed this admission with "How can I stop It?" I reminded her that she had been expressing envy for people such as Jacqueline Kennedy, whom she saw as frivolous, vain and able to enjoy seeking pleasure, and that she might try, rather than getting rid of these inclinations in herself, to accept them, to relish them, indulge them by going to the beauty parlor more often, for example. The same approach was used with her when she talked about her vindictiveness. She did not immediately stop her obsessive self-pitying reporting of hurts but this approach has given us a tool with which to shorten the amount of time wasted in this way. Obviously this latter approach is an application of Wenkart's concept of "self-acceptance" as well as Frankl's "paradoxical intention."

Physical Encounters

Louise is an exceptionally beautiful young aspiring actress who discovered that she had multiple sclerosis three months after her marriage, one year before beginning therapy. She has been seen in group therapy for about one year, having entered therapy to obtain help with her unhappy marital situation and her life-long morbid dependency. Louise reports to the group that she has been so depressed and withdrawn that she has been unable, or unwilling, to leave her apartment for one month. She had started to come to the group session the previous week but had turned back after reaching my door fearing a "confrontation," she said. She tells the group that she feels she has "something" which wants to come out but all efforts to help her verbalize her feelings lead to nothing except greater withdrawal from the group. In fact, after the session had progressed for about one half hour, Louise is slumped on the couch with a blank, far away expression on her face.

Sandra, after trying to draw her out for about five minutes, wonders if the "confrontation" which Louise feared and wanted might not be a physical one. She would like Louise to sit up straight since this in itself might change her mood, Sandra feels. Louise's reaction is a helplessly stubborn one—"I can't move." I suggest to Louise that she take responsibility and express directly what she is doing. I also suggest that she say "I won't" instead of "I can't." She finally says, "I won't move, fuck you." Sandra says that she will make Louise sit up. Louise, avoiding any "cop out" on the basis of her spasticity or presumed weakness from the multiple sclerosis, says with some anger, "No, you won't." Then, to the group's surprise, Louise manages, for ten minutes to prevent Sandra from pulling her up. In the process Louise snarls and looks with hatred at Sandra as the latter uses all her strength in trying to straighten her up. No words are spoken during this grappling encounter, except for the group members, surprised comments such as "God, you're so strong Louise!" and "You come over so helpless and weak."

Finally, Sandra conceded that Louise had won and that she could not be straightened up. At this point, to her own surprise, Louise announced with awe and amusement: "Now I *feel* like sitting up straight!" She proceeded to do so, became lively, and exclaimed "I had never believed in these physical encounters before, but the effect is amazing!" Again, the group members commented on her strength which she covers by withdrawing and appearing weak and helpless. She was emotionally involved during the rest of the session and left with an entirely different spirit than she had experienced for one month. Soon afterwards she felt the courage to leave her cruel, detached and impotent husband, feeling strong enough to manage on her own.

What are the elements that led to this effect? Some might say that the concern and attention of the group and the desire to please them by changing had led to Louise's moving from a helpless, sullen role to an active, lively one. But the group had unsuccessfully tried all kinds of encouragement verbally, including reassuring, analyzing her behavior ("in withdrawal you can keep your fantasy of being a great, undiscovered actress"), taunting her (in an effort to make her angry) and sharing their experiences by telling her what they were trying to express when they withdrew from contact with the world, from competition, etc. None of these approaches had begun to move Louise.

It was certainly not only the interest of the group that led to her breakthrough. Perhaps it was some elemental contact with her own feelings and with another human being. Sandra later described that fight as being like two little girls having a stubborn battle of wills.

"Winning was important," Louise said. The groups' sanction and admiration for her effort and strength was a supportive element but her own feeling of the power of her stubbornness was undoubtedly most important. I can think of no other way she could have experienced this in a more direct and satisfying manner than through this physical confrontation.

Obviously, these confrontations are not panaceas. Often, they have little or no effect on participants—except perhaps to pave the way for further interaction. For example, Louise commented that a previous physical match ("pressing," as described by Schutz, 1969) had not moved her at all.

Dream Interpretation, Gestalt Techniques

Perls has taught us that it is important to let patients play the *objects* in a dream as well as the persons. Even if a patient says he had a dream but can't remember it, he may be asked to "play the dream which you are blocking from your memory." He may be encouraged to have a dialogue with his dream and say lines such as "Dream, I won't let you come into the front of my mind." Speaking as the elusive dream he may then say something like "I'm very vague and slippery. I won't let you get hold of me." Of course, the therapist will have the patient repeat these words, listen to himself and apply them to his whole being if he has not already done so. Often, he will then remember a significant dream.

A 60-year-old, self-effacing writer who considered himself very youthful and was concerned about his impotence and lack of interest in his writing, dreamed of a narrow street with people trying to get into an open window in order to look down on something. Asked to "be the street" he responded, "I'm very happy that all these curious, happy people are climbing all over me—I am a very old and festive street." When asked if he heard himself, he recognized immediately that he was feeling not only that people were stepping all over him but that he experienced in himself a rather ripe joyousness. Although he had entered the session feeling very depressed and heavy, he left with a light feeling after experiencing these and other feelings. Obviously, a large element of suggestion (hypnosis?) was instrumental in my asking him to focus on the festive feeling as well as the stepped-on feeling.

In a group Gladys, a suicidal spinster of 46 years of age, states that she had dreamed she was being buried alive. "I put the first shovelful of dirt into my mouth then everybody heaped dirt on me until I was buried." I suggest that she lie down in the middle of the floor and be dead. Then I suggest that shovelful after shovelful of dirt are being piled on her. Another group member, Beatrice, suddenly cries out: "I feel the dirt on my face—in my nose! I can't breathe."

I hold Beatrice as she cries and gasps repeating in a frightened voice, "I can't breathe!" I ask her to "Tell me what's stopping you!" She chokes out, "All the phoniness, all those years of holding in my feelings, never saying what I feel." I suggest "Say *one* thing you feel right now and you'll be able to breathe." "All I can think is 'fuck'" ... "Say it," I demand. "Fuck." "Again" "Fuck" ("louder") Fuck, fuck, fuck!" she screams. "I'm not like these people! I don't feel like them! They all hate their parents. I *like* my mother and father!" ("You don't have to be like them. You *have* your own feelings. It's *alright* not to hate your parents," I comment.) Her breathing becomes deeper and I say "That's it, let it in and out, enjoy the air." She becomes calm and returns to her seat. She asks me if she should tell all her feelings to people. I suggest that she keep some in reserve. She agrees. She is beginning to learn an inner control, to replace her myriad of "shoulds." Incidentally, within the two months following her experience of playing dead, Gladys, for the first time in her adult life experienced and showed definite signs of being alive. She showed facial animation, extreme restlessness and started to talk about and experiment with being in her terms "naughty." For example, she dieted, bought clothes, and she took a four-day trip to Copenhagen.

In the above incident we see again the value of "acting out" a dream as well as the emotional contagion which is often seen in such dramatic enactments. The careful suggestive control required of the therapist is also clearly demonstrated.

Hypnotic Experiences in Encounter Groups

Towards the end of a 24-hour marathon Jane, who in ten years of therapy with two analysts had never enjoyed her sexuality, volunteers to sit in the "hot seat." Suddenly she turns toward me and begins to punch viciously at the pillow which I am holding in my lap. She screams out "You goddam bastard! You cocksucking son of a bitch!" and hits even harder, so hard that as I hold the pillow in front of me, she almost knocks my chair over. I ask her "What are you hitting, Jane?" "My father's penis!" she yells. I let her continue hitting and shouting in a frenzy, for about five minutes more.

I suggest to her that she act out a dialogue with her father, playing both parts herself. She explains that he would speak In Yiddish, but she does not speak Yiddish. I tell her, "I will translate." For her father, she then says "I am sorry" ("Enschuldlg mir," I translate). "I'm in pain" ("Es tut mlr vey"). For herself she screams her resentment towards him. I then suggest "It's time, Jane that you forgive your father. He's an old man now and you are grown up." I hand her the pillow. "Here, hold him and talk to him. You are the strong one now." She rocks the pillow, cries and talks to her father. "Does he hear you?" I ask. "Yes." Suddenly Jane turns to me "Let me hold your head." I do so and she lays my head against her breast. She cries out, "Daddy, feel my breasts! I'm a grown woman! I'm going to go out and find a man like you ... and I'm GOING TO FUCK HIM!"

I suggest that she express her feelings toward some man in the audience. She assumes a patrician pose and after a dramatic silence of two minutes commands "Donald, come here." Donald, who later admitted that he was quaking in his boots after seeing her violent display, approaches her cautiously. "Hold me, Donald," she commands. "Protect me!" Donald embraces her while many members in the audience weep.

Subsequent to this marathon she was able in weekly group sessions to act out sexual and other conflicts, employing role-playing similar to that which I have described above. She reported enjoyable sexual experiences, was able to sustain a relationship with one man for a year (for the first time in her life) and then married him.

Now, this type of drama occurs very often in encounter and Gestalt groups. It is brought out without any formal hypnotic induction and with minimal suggestions of any kind. Yet when the patient is told "Talk to your father," she talks as if he were really there. When asked "Do you see him?" she will answer in the affirmative. Thus, hallucinatory behavior is demonstrated. If this were seen after a hypnotic induction the patient would be judged to be in a state of about Grade 10 hypnosis—a hypnogogic trance with positive auditory and visual hallucinations (Hilgard, 1965).

We see that. under certain conditions—the presence of an expectant audience, heightened emotional tension, the verbal expression of certain emotion-laden feelings and attitudes in the present tense, the presence of a trusted leader or guide—a person is more prone to wipe out the boundary between an "as if" perceiving and a "real" one. For example, by talking to her father. Jane soon felt and perceived that he "really" was there. Now, in the example given, Jane was able after 23 hours in the marathon to eliminate this boundary by saying the words and throwing herself into the role of a child. In other cases, the addition of more conventional "hypnotic" suggestions or "hypnotic" induction might have made the elimination of the boundary more feasible or more acceptable to certain patients. Barber's work in trying to define what conditions are necessary to attain this state of mind, is potentially helpful. although experienced clinicians develop a "feel" for the types of settings and suggestions of time of voice to use in "setting the scene" and eliciting the desired behavior. Sometimes their directions are labelled as "hypnotic inductions." At other times the patient, mostly by himself, will enter into a revivification of old experiences or an increased awareness of body sensations. The latter behavior may be in response to the conditions I have outlined or to pre-existing conditions—expectations and auto-suggestions of the patient himself.

Influencing Patients—Inevitable and Helpful

Whether the final behavior of the patient is labelled as being "in hypnosis" or not is rather unimportant. What *is* important is having the greatest possible awareness. And, thus, control of what we as therapists are contributing to the situation. In the analytic situation, it is only a rare hold-out who will claim that we do not influence our patients. When we comment, we influence; when we remain silent, we influence; when we are with the patient in a Park Avenue office, we influence. Perhaps it is only more obvious to note that when we swim with him in a hot spring pool in the nude, we also influence.

As clinician and as scientist it behooves us to examine and study the *nature* of this influence, to direct it in more effective, most helpful and most efficient directions. For example, we can help patients to learn inner control of emotions by encouraging them to experience and express their feelings and thoughts in the most open, most intense manner possible. In this way they will feel their own organismic limitations. Those who fear losing control will find that they do not fall apart or destroy others when they express the full extent of their vindictiveness or rage in a therapeutic setting. Often it is more possible for them to do this first by role playing, then by relating to the actual persons in the therapy group. Only after they have had the *experience* of letting go can they be encouraged to control their feelings and words or to direct them in an effective way towards actual people such as those in their therapy group. After a person has acted out his protective feelings towards his mother, for example, he may be asked to express the same feeling towards some of the women in the group.

A woman who was furious with the other women in her group, and subsequently evoked hostile responses from them, was encouraged to express her fury towards her mother first. She did this initially in an uncontrolled, vicious manner. After playing both her own role and that of her mother, the degree of viciousness subsided and she was able to fantasize being constructively critical of her mother. At this point, I suggested that she criticize the women in the group again and she was able to do it in a manner which enabled *them* to listen without retaliatory viciousness of their own.

Whether or not we throw out the word "hypnosis" because of the many mystical and charlatan associations of the word, is not, it seems to me nearly so important as whether or not we become more aware of the many factors which influence our patients and our own responses and behavior, including our taking responsibility for and accepting the fact that we influence our patients, hopefully for the good. The concept of Svengali like influence has long been discarded in hypnosis and the illusion that psychoanalysis can be value-free has been quite thoroughly destroyed in recent years, partly due to Horney's pioneer thinking as expressed in her chapter "A Morality of Evolution" (Horney 1950).

Experience—Not Talking About

We have techniques. We have goals. Perls and others have spelled out, in their development of Gestalt therapy, many techniques which we can relate directly to our goals, without needing to rely on rather vague general constructs such as "self-realization" even though these may still be useful in retroactively evaluating the longer-range picture. For example, in groups, if a patient has experienced himself differently, he shows it immediately, in his voice, in the way his face clears, in his perceptions of others in the group. He may be directed, and often is, to look at the others and asked "Do you see them?" When the veil of his confusion and alienation is drawn aside, he is often surprised at the vividness with which he sees people and objects.

Patient's Responsibilities and Involvement in Planning Treatment

Since one of the prime goals in my existentially-rooted therapy, and Gestalt therapy in particular, is the insistence that the patient assume responsibility for himself as much as possible, it is natural that I carry this attitude into asking the patient, as soon as possible, to decide important questions with regard to his therapy.

After a first consultation session, I will generally ask a patient whether he found the session helpful, whether he is more or less comfortable at the end than at the beginning, whether he feels that he would like one or more sessions further before trying to decide whether he finds our working together helpful. If he counters with the non-responsible "You are the doctor and I'd like you to tell me whether you can help me," I may tell him my feelings of hopefulness or lack of it based on my response to him, my past experience and so on, and then I will still leave it up to him to decide whether he wants to invest the time and money for another session. I may, on the other hand, suggest that he play Dr. Rosen and, as me, respond to his questions.

For example, Daniel, a rather paranoid 40-year-old man, spent most of his first session telling me how stupid, rigid or self-seeking all his other therapists had been and concluded with his considered and frank opinion that there really was no therapy that could help him with his problems of indecisiveness, helpless rage at his wife and multiple somatic preoccupations. He had come to me for hypnotic therapy after hearing me discuss hypnosis on a television program. In this first session, since this was what he had come for, I suggested that we test his response to hypnosis. Since I perceived that he was obviously very much afraid of being influenced by anyone I told him this and suggested that I would show him how I hypnotize myself and that he could try the same method with himself if he so chose. He discovered that, after concentrating on a button on my couch, maintaining the image in his mind and letting his eyes close, he felt that he was in a sort of trance. But the fact that astounded both of us was that in this state, no matter what we called it, he was a different person. He focused on *himself,* *his* fantasies, *his* memories, *his* fears, instead of me, his wife, career decisions and other outside factors. From a bitter paranoid with a forced supercilious smile he changed to a serious, thoughtful, very sensitive person—rather objective about himself and quite poetic in his choice of fantasies.

At the end of the session, after emerging from his "trance," he challenged me in his usual guarded manner, asking if I thought I could help him. I simply reflected my observations on the differences I have noted above. I told him that with his long history of refractoriness to all treatments, I had strong doubts about his being able to make significant changes and yet that I was also impressed by his persistence in seeking this type of help. I told him that I liked working with him when he was in the self-hypnotized state and he agreed that he was fascinated also to find that he was able to bring out such fantasy resources in himself. I cut my usual fee to accommodate his finances and he declared that he wanted to come once a week. Whenever he would ask me, as he had his previous therapists, whether I thought he was getting anything out of therapy, I would tell him my observations, usually emphasizing the negative slightly. He would then assure me that "somehow" he felt he was making some progress. His wife's therapist, he finally told me, had noted a big improvement in him.

Dangers of Encounter Groups

Any technique, used mechanically and without a place in some broader conceptions of aims, goals and understanding of the person's character structure, can be ineffective at best and growth blocking at worst. The danger of "addiction" to dramatic encounter meetings exists with some patients. However, some analysts—frightened or shocked by some of the more dramatic and bizarre reports emanating from the thousands of "encounter groups," professional and amateur, may be disinclined to utilize some of the gimmicks—even in the context of an ongoing relationship—with the background of their own professional experience and ethical goals to protect the patients.

Some analysts have been concerned, and rightly so, with the danger of encouraging highly emotional people to express all of their suppressed and repressed rage, despair, or clinging needs in a concentrated manner and in a comparatively brief period of time. It is in precisely this area where our experience with hypnosis is invaluable. We have learned, in working with hypnotized persons that a simple suggestion will often stop an emotional outburst just as quickly as it may start one. I will give an example.

Seymour, a 55-year-old anxious hypochondriacal married man, with married children, had been in therapy with various therapists for over 15 years, with no improvement in his chronic anxiety and somatic preoccupation. He had, in his fourth group session with me, spent half an hour and had exhausted himself, shouting hoarsely at his long dead parents. He is short of breath, feeling weak, perspiring profusely. The group, as an audience, have been awed and impressed by the strength of the emotion and the voice coming from this man who they had originally perceived as a sniveling coward. I recall that after his last outburst of anger in the group he had gone to his father's grave, telling father that he wanted to pee on him. At the next group session, he had reported being subsequently very depressed for three days. He doubted the therapeutic value of this suffering and threatened to leave therapy. I decide to help him towards some degree of closure before he leaves my office, this time. First, I suggest that he play his father, after he has finished expressing his remaining anger at his father. Later, I highlight both his father's and his own areas of strength. Finally, I encourage him to express his strength with members of the group. In "Gestalt" terms I am helping him "complete the Gestalt" by owning and identifying with both the "father" and the "child" in himself. In hypnotic terms I am, indirectly, giving him positive, reassuring suggestions to counteract his self-hate. This time there is no reactive guilt, but instead he follows the session with a period of increased energy and productivity.

Conclusion

I would like to propose the following basic principles about therapy.

1. The therapist must conduct the therapy or else no therapy takes place. As Horney and others have put it, patients come into therapy to enhance,

repair and improve their neuroses. It is our job to redirect them towards growth and self-realization.
2. Patients are most open to therapeutic changes in an atmosphere of strong involvement—involvement of the patient with his own feelings and thoughts, involvement between patient and therapist. In groups, this intense involvement may occur between patients. Patients move best when they are moved. I would include here the experience of feeling "intellectually" stimulated.

With the recognition of those factors, the technical problems in therapy could be seen as revolving around first finding more effective means of enhancing involvement while the theoretical problems evolve around determining which values and goals are best aimed at and encouraged. With regard to the latter, the questions must constantly be asked by therapist and patient: "What am I being cured to as well as what am I being cured of?"

Karen Horney's holistic theory of psychoanalysis, with its clarification of character defenses such as intellectualizing and externalizing, and with its integrated emphasis on factors such as alienation, neurotic pride and "shoulds" provides me with answers to the latter question. The existentialists' highlighting of the importance of choice, awareness, responsibility, wholeness, process and risking, point up directions for goals. Fritz Perls provides invaluable aids in solving the technical problems. He suggests many new ways of "being with the patient" and thus following Horney's injunction for conducting an analysis.

Discussion

Martin Kasson, Ed.D., President, Council of Psychoanalytic Psychotherapy; Morton Prince Clinic for Hypnotherapy.

It appears that the disagreement this evening is going to have to come from the audience rather than from the discussants so ... without asking Dr. Rosen's permission I am going to discuss his paper as if it were titled "The desirability of exposing yourself to various new non-psychoanalytic therapeutic modalities and incorporating those compatible with your personality and therapeutic orientation into a sound psychoanalytic framework and then if necessary giving good reasons for doing so." One can raise many theoretically valid or perhaps pedantically provocative questions about Dr. Rosen's case illustrations and some of his dynamic hypotheses but I don't believe these are relevant here this evening although perhaps some other time they might be. What is relevant is that Dr. Rosen has stated that, without renouncing his psychoanalytic framework and heritage he has been adventuresome, brave or whatever other words we may ascribe to him, and has exposed himself to these various new techniques, gimmicks—if we want to use that somewhat contrived word—and found the ones, that for him, seem to work better and faster in reaching people. Now he has more or less specifically chosen to focus on five of these although he has really only discussed three. May I point out that he takes for granted group therapy and the marathon and doesn't even mention a discussion of these although they are really new modalities, not perhaps as new as some of the others and in certain psychoanalytic circles are still frowned upon very strongly.

I would like very briefly to give our discussion a historical perspective, that I think will be helpful. In essence there have been three main psychological forces to date, or currents if you wish: the first was the behaviorist—shades of Pavlov and Skinner and certainly a resurgence of this approach with the works of Wolpe and others. Now we are not here to discuss the values and the pros and cons of behavior therapy, but I do think that it behooves us to at least be aware of what they are doing and from my own experience to not belittle their effectiveness especially in work of phobic desensitization with people who are afraid of taking airplane trips and problems of that nature. Now certainly the second current was psychoanalysis and we could spend evenings discussing or perhaps arguing as to which therapeutic modalities are even qualified to be considered as psychoanalytic. The third force is the one identified as the humanistic and that's a new and rather broad one. It's usually identified with the writings of Maslow, the later Carl Rogers, Alan Watts and many others. But in terms of therapeutic schools there are perhaps three main ones, although under the umbrella of humanistic psychology many new therapies and many old-timers with perhaps new faces are emerging and Dr. Rosen has mentioned a few of these. Under the humanistic category the three outstanding schools are first: the existential. I don't believe there's anyone in this room who has not been to some extent exposed and influenced by the existential. I know I have been but I'm not quite sure how and I'm not quite sure how I've incorporated it into my therapeutic practice. And it may be my limitation but I really had trouble with those long German unending sentences and paragraphs. The second school is one that I would venture to guess that many of you are not even aware of. And that is Logotherapy of Victor Frankl which is considered the third school of Vienna. And at least you ought to know about it.

Now the third therapeutic school, and to me the most important, and I believe to Dr. Rosen in the emphasis that he has placed on it, is that of Gestalt therapy. It should be noted that Fritz Perls wrote his first book on Gestalt therapy thirty years ago; "Ego, Hunger and Aggression" and then the "Gestalt Therapy" with Paul Goodman and Hefferline, was written some 25 years ago. But it was not until his work at Esalen and with the emergence of "Gestalt Therapy, Verbatim" that Gestalt therapy has really come into the fore. Now Dr. Rosen is to be admired for his rather effective efforts to try to give this group an orientation to something as complicated and powerful as Gestalt therapy in 60 easy minutes. I was going to take him to task for not at least advising you to read "Gestalt Therapy Verbatim," but he has modified his paper since and suggested it. For those of you that haven't I certainly urge that you at least read it and then perhaps follow it up with an exposure to a Gestalt therapy workshop. It's an experiential therapy and reading about it really doesn't do it. It's experiencing it that counts.

Regarding hypnosis as a modality, I don't believe, Dr. Rosen, that you have to be omnipotent to be a hypnotist. I see some of my senior colleagues from the Morton Prince Clinic here, and perhaps we can call on them to speak a little bit about hypnosis. It's a modality that's been around for some time. If a certain colleague of ours had taken a different bent, I imagine all of us would have had to be effective hypnotists or we couldn't even be psychoanalysts. But it didn't work that way. Now hypnosis is a modality that can be used in many different therapeutic schools and Dr. Rosen has given examples, rather interesting effective ones, of some of the different ways that hypnosis can be used. Perhaps some of my colleagues might want to comment about some of the other ways that hypnosis is used in different therapeutic contexts. The behaviorists use hypnosis. And, because it has been shunted to the sidelines, it has the disadvantage that there are many less than ethical people using it and using it potently and effectively, ethically or otherwise. I think Dr. Rosen has nobly, yet effectively, attempted to orient you to some of the controversies and questions debated by the various schools and factions that exist in the hypnotic world. For those of you who haven't, I might suggest you read even as simple a book as *Hypnosis—Fact and Fiction* and then expose yourself to a hypnotic experience. It's a very powerful one.

Now encounter is a catch-all term and a multitude of sins have been carried out under the guise and the term of encounter. It has taken on for some people a stigma and perhaps rightly so, but that does not invalidate the positive things that have emerged from encounter. In a sense it had its birth out in Esalen with the work of Schutz and the other innovators. Much of the encounter techniques were worked out in the marathon setting, with the exploration and experiences of Mintz and others. And even Hollywood, made that famous movie about Bob and Ted and Carol and Alice and everybody else. The encounter movement gave birth to many of the touching involvements that were previously so taboo in psychoanalytic circles. In addition, many of the contributions to the field of humanistic psychology have come from fields other than those that we ordinarily recognize as the psychotherapeutic ones perhaps because they were not as limited and constricted by the frameworks in which they operated, from theater and from dance have come many important contributions in terms of some of the encounter techniques. This is also true for many other settings; art, music, etc. What we have seen as a result of this humanistic current or force, is the emergence of the interests in the work of which Dr. Rosen spoke. That is, the integration of the mind and body, following up on the work of many including Wilhelm Reich. The school of Bioenergetic Analysis, as carried out by Alexander Lowen and John Pierrakos, is a leading example.

There are many, many other therapeutic modalities some of which may be what you might call a flash in the pan, that are here today and gone tomorrow. And, as Dr. Rosen has indicated, perhaps for many of these only time will tell and evaluate. But they at least are worth knowing about, and perhaps exposing yourself to. Take the word and experience of people that you respect—if they say, "hey, this is worth seeing," at least do so. Just to mention a few briefly. Dr. Rose and Dr. Rosen both spoke of Moreno's technique of psychodrama. It's an old-timer. It's been around. But it is emerging with a new force. And it does have something to offer. Dr. Rosen spoke of Eric Berne, without really expanding to some degree his contribution in terms of transactional analysis. Most of us know Berne through his all too popular *Games People Play*. But he has written on a more serious level in *Transactional Analysis*. His work is worthwhile seeing and reading. And even, as someone suggested, if you extract only three new therapeutic sentences, it may be worthwhile. There's the work of Albert Pesso, who comes from the dance department, in terms of psycho-motor therapy. There's the work of Alex Rubin, who comes from the theater, with encounter techniques. And I could go on like this. But, in essence what we are saying, and Dr. Rosen really said it so well, is, to paraphrase a noted President, not everything works for everybody all the time, but the more numerous the therapeutic modalities you have available that are a genuine intrinsic part of you, that are real for you, the more you have that may be able to reach a patient who in the past has gone on to know all the correct answers without anything really, really being corrected.

Note

1 This chapter was presented at the December 3, 1970 meeting of the Association for the Advancement of Psychoanalysis, and was previously published in the *American Journal of Psychoanalysis*, 1972, vol. 32(1), pp. 90–102.

References

Barber, T.X. (1967). *Hypnosis: A Scientific Approach*. New York: Van Nostrand Reinhold Company.
Enright, J.B. (1967). *Awareness Training in Mental Health Professions*. In *Gestalt Therapy Now* (pp. 263–273). Gouldsboro, ME: The Gestalt Journal Press.
Haley, J. (1967). *Advanced Techniques of Hypnosis and Therapy. Selected papers of Milton H. Erickson*. New York: Grune & Stratton.
Hilgard, E.R., (1965). *Hypnotic Susceptibility*. New York: Harcourt, Brace & World.
Horney, K. (1950). *Neurosis and Human Growth*. New York: W. W. Norton.
Kamlya, J. (1969). Operant Control of the EEG Alpha Rhythm and Some of Its Reported Effects on Consciousness. In Charles T. Tart (ed.) *Altered States of Consciousness*, pp. 507–518. New York: John Wiley & Sons.
Naranjo, C. (1967). Present-Centeredness: Technique, Prescription and Ideal. In J. Fagan, and I.L. Shepherd (eds) *Gestalt Therapy Now*, pp. 47–69. Palo Alto: Science and Behavior Books.
Orne, M.T. (1967). The Nature of Hypnosis: Artifact and Essence. *Journal of Abnormal and Social Psychology*, 58(3): 277–299.
Perls, F.S. (1969). *Gestalt Therapy Verbatim*. Lafayette: Real People Press.

Perls, F.S. (1970). *Four Lectures*. In J. Fagan, and I.L. Shepherd (eds) *Gestalt Therapy Now*, pp. 9–10. Palo Alto: Science and Behavior Books.

Raginsky, B.B. (1962). Sensory hypnoplasty with case illustrations. *International Journal of Clinical and Experimental Hypnosis*, 10: 205–219.

Sacerdote, P. (1967). Therapeutic Use of Induced Dreams. *American Journal of Clinical Hypnosis*, 10(1): 1–9.

Schutz, W. (1969). *Joy*. New York: Grove.

9

THE EVOCATIVE POWER OF LANGUAGE[1]

Introduction

This chapter is a part of Kay Thompson's *Collected Works*. Kay Thompson was a dentist who was one of Erickson's patients; she was also a noted therapist who worked with Erickson's techniques and wrote about them. She was one of Erickson's primary students and teachers of his techniques.

When you were with her, everything she said and did had therapeutic intent. She would talk about the back of the brain and the front of the brain as if she could just ask them to do their job and bring out the power of the unconscious. I can't convey how powerful she was, or do justice to her artistry. The impact of her technique was very powerful. She said she did this by thinking before she spoke. She spelled out things that Erickson did but which he didn't spell out, like his use of reframing.

My commentary on the "Evocative Power of Language" discusses Kay's approaches. I noted that Kay and Milton had common elements in their use of metaphors and post-hypnotic suggestions. Kay Thompson delivered things differently than Erickson, whose stories focused on anthropology and family stories. Kay talked less about other people and more about her own interests.

Kay Thompson used a lot of word play, talking about "that void which you have avoided filling." She related to the patient's problems. When patients had pain, she used a common technique Erickson used: she changed the pain, transferring the tension from a jaw to a clenched fist. She then suggested that whenever a patient had pain, he could clench his fist and feel the tightness.

The main difference between Kay Thompson and Erickson was that she liked to play with words a lot. Her work is a good example of conversational inductions. Conversational inductions are "interspersed suggestions" aimed at suggesting things like trusting yourself, distorting your time perceptions to suit your own needs. She would say things like, "You have all the time that you need in the time that's available." She didn't say, "I will hypnotize you and then you will do something;" instead, her suggestions were conversational because they were put in almost casually, as in conversations. But every word that was spoken was aimed at guiding patients into dealing with issues of their living needs, involving taking and letting go of control, for example.

She had a joy in playing with words and an expectation that subjects could do what she asked.

Kay Thompson talked as if we are always in a trance of some kind and she tried to change the trance from one that could be symptomatic to one in which more positive responses could emerge.

***

While conducting therapy or teaching, Kay Thompson would say, "Not a word passes my lips before I have thought of it first." When I heard this statement in a workshop, I found it hard to understand. I knew that she did not mean that she was obsessing on or even consciously naming each word that she spoke. That would have slowed her verbalizations almost to a halt. I realized that the "thinking" must occur on an unconscious level. After reading instructions to her musician friend in Chapter 22 it was clear to me that she utilized time distortion in the same way that she instructed him to do.

Kay frequently taught that, "I believe that everything that I say, once the patient walks in that door into my office, is leading toward the ultimate goal." So, we have evidence that Kay was methodically/meticulously processing her language on multiple levels. One was incorporating orientation toward the goal, sometimes including preplanning exactly what she was going to say, as in her work with patients in acute pain situations. At the same time, she was utilizing trance in several ways. She openly described developing an intense interpersonal trance for accessing her and her client's unconscious process. And she utilized time distortion during her communication, to scan what she was saying prior to speaking.

In general, Kay's approach to therapy and to teaching (she tended to equate them) was relatively simple—even as it was hidden and decorated through her brilliant and creative use of words, images and nonverbal communications. It is mostly an injunctive approach. She prepares her patients and students by directing their attention toward their own "knowing and power" even as she presents examples, images, and metaphors to "jump start" their inner searching so that they can find resources to apply to their concerns and needs. She suggests, "So you already know everything you need to know about how to increase your circulation to carry the oxygen and nutrients to heal the parts of your body that need to heal." Then, just to make sure that he knows, she repeats previous suggestions: "You know how to make that happen by thinking warm to carry that flush ... to carry oxygen into that area ... to carry away waste products."

Unlike Erickson, who almost always answered questions with another story or metaphor, Kay often explains her interventions in relatively simple terms. In Chapter 22, for example, she points out that she used metaphors of climbing, the growth of a flower and the utilization of "pebbles," or blockages on the path to augment growth and mastery. She notes that she induced relaxation with the imagery of a swimming pool and the warming sun. The depth of searching was tied to getting into the water with the recurring question, "How deep do I want to go?"

As Erickson did in his story, "Dry Beds" (Rosen, 1982), Kay adds directives for reinforcement. Erickson had instructed, "You can practice starting and stopping, starting and stopping." Kay says, "When you practice relaxation, practice imagining taking a walk to the swimming pool or taking a walk beside the river. You can tune in to the ability to relax and produce your own endorphins and enkephalins, your own interferon." She might preface an injunction with a phrase intended to bring the communication down to the level of a child. For example, she explains (Chapter 22) that she introduced more complex language after "protecting it" by saying "it *really doesn't matter* whether the front of your mind hears it." Erickson might have appealed to the child by inducing regression and talking as an adult to a child, telling corny jokes or speaking in simple language.

It is obvious that Kay and Milton shared some very common elements in their work—the use of metaphors, reframing and posthypnotic suggestions. However, they were quite different in their content and delivery. For example, Erickson's stories tended to be at least a step removed from him, referring, for example, to anthropological facts, experiences with previous patients, and most closely to family tales, all presented with mild amusement. In fact, tape recordings of his last years are punctuated by repeated laughter, which caused him to cough frequently. On the other hand, Kay's stories are more likely to refer to her own interests and experience and they tend to be presented seriously, often using poetic language.

Instead of directly ordering or even suggesting certain skills, Kay will gently, almost casually, suggest them, as in Chapter 22: "You need to get in touch with the fact that you now can learn to use the switches that carry the feeling pain to that part of your body that you want to control." She then presents the example of a rheostat "to know whether it's safe to turn it all the way off."

In her treatment of temporomandibular pain Kay clearly illustrates her practice of turning destructive into constructive and perpetuating the result with posthypnotic suggestions. First, she has her subject transfer tension into a clenched fist. Then she says, "Every time your jaws come together ... there's going to be an automatic signal ... electric current ... into your hands ... clench your fist." She has previously pointed out that while clenching the jaws is destructive, clenching the fist builds up forearm muscles for swimming or playing tennis. Finally, she suggests, "When that stress is coming back, you can use ... the same clenched fist and tightness."

In Chapter 24, Kay's word play is extensive and especially rich (e.g. "that void that you have avoided filling"). In this chapter, as in the other chapters on clinical demonstrations, her conversational inductions and trances include innumerable "interspersed suggestions." They are so continuous that "interspersed" is an inaccurate term. Everything that Kay says in these sessions, including her questions, constitutes suggestions regarding multiple subjects, including trusting yourself, distorting time perceptions to suit your needs, to living today and to taking and letting go of control. And she adds, "It was all posthypnotic suggestion work from my frame of reference." Her unique way of delivering suggestions is marked by her obvious joy in playing with words and her open-eyed enthusiasm and expectation that her subjects can do the things she asks.

There is so much to be learned from these chapters, not only about how to do therapy, but, on a deeper level, about how to conduct one's life. As expressed in Chapter 24, Kay's comment about control was especially meaningful to me.

> It's only the people who don't have control who have to have it all the time to be sure they don't lose it. When you are sure you really have it, you don't need it because you can get it anytime you want it.

Like Kay, I often look at life as moving from one kind of "trance" to another. As she indicates in Chapter 24, therapy can help a patient "to come out of the trance he was in, in order to have the opportunity to go into another trance."

It is impossible to summarize the artistry of Kay's therapeutic communications, unique style, and her ways of maximizing the evocative power of words. Reading and rereading the transcripts in this section will help people to get a feeling for Kay's special style and creativity and the variety of ways she utilizes the power of language. Readers will undoubtedly try to imitate her at first, adapting her examples to their own work.

But in order to truly emulate Kay Thompson, and indirectly, Erickson, I believe that we need to enter into a "therapizing" or a "teaching trance," in which we focus on the needs of our patient or student, ask ourselves what the situation calls for and trust our unconscious mind to guide us in guiding and encouraging his or her growth and healing. When we do this, we can tap into and utilize appropriate material from our life experiences and from the rigorous practice and training Kay so consistently emphasized as necessary to feed our unconscious. Like Kay, we must always be aware of the evocative power of words, because hypnotherapy is fundamentally a process of healing with language.

Note

1 Previously published in *The Art of Therapeutic Communication, The Collected Works of Kay F. Thompson,* 2004, edited by Saralee Kane, MSW and Karen Olness M.D., as commentary, pp. 366–370.

Reference

Rosen, S. (ed.) (1982). *"My Voice Will Go with You": The Teaching Tales of Milton Erickson.* New York: Norton.

10

THE FEBRUARY MAN FOREWORD[1]

Introduction

The chapter that follows is about corrective regression experiences, which involve regressing back to an experience and then putting something into the memory that changes or corrects it. Simply understanding the past does not change or correct the past.

Corrective regression at first involves bringing back the memory as it was remembered but then going back and looking at it in a way that would be good for it to be remembered, a way which is not the actual memory but involves a helpful reframing. That helpful way is what I call a corrected way.

In *The February Man*, the patient had a fear of swimming and blamed herself for her sister's near drowning. Erickson placed an inhibition on her swimming and then withdrew the inhibition at the next session. By placing the inhibition, she was able to have a corrective experience; when he withdrew his correction for the inhibition; the corrective experience was still remembered.

It was important that she experienced the corrective experience in the regressed state since that was the state in which she had the inhibition in the first place, so when he was able to change it in that state, the result was carried on even when she came out of that state.

When I regress people to childhood, I tell them that they are younger. You're not 55 years old, you're eight years old, you think like eight years old, you feel like eight years old, and you are eight years old. I say, "You are eight years old," not "You remember being eight years old." I will ask patients to confirm the fact that they have a feeling that they are eight years old by describing more details about their situation at age eight. For example, are they outside or inside, is there any furniture near them, and I ask then to describe the furniture. I have them describe all these things in the present tense, not as remembered but as happening right now.

That's the regression, and once they can have the experience and it feels like it's going on right now, then the changes that are suggested to them also feel like they are more real. Corrective regression is simply regression and then correction.

Another corrective technique would be to experience thoughts and feelings by reframing them. Reframing results in a corrective experience. How did the patient in the February Man reframe her feelings of guilt about wanting to kill her sister? First, she recognized that she is condemning herself for her sister's death. To reframe that, Erickson adds other elements to the experience, the element of seeing this self-condemnation as only a small part of her experience, and not important. He helps her expand the experience. And that's how she reframed self-condemnation as a step on the path to self-understanding. Similarly, Erickson reframed sibling rivalry because remembering the experience as jealousy did not allow the child to experience her whole experience. She needed to look at her jealousy and other aspects of the experience, such as the value of a child's appreciating her own worth.

When Erickson hypnotized me on another occasion, he asked what I would like help with. I said I wanted help with my tendency to intellectualize. He told me, "You can continue to intellectualize but intellectualize in a different way." He modeled a different form of intellectualizing by wondering. He never said instead of "intellectualizing you can wonder." Instead, he left it for me to look at the intellectualizing in a different way, I found myself wondering. Instead of blaming myself for intellectualizing, I was able to wonder. Although he role-modeled a different type of intellectualizing by introducing the idea of wonderment, he left it up to me to make the connection on my own.

He always left it up to the patient to make the connection. He presented it as a possibility and left it up to me to adapt the attitude of wondering. As Erickson said, "It is the patient who does the work. All that the therapist does is to provide conditions in which this work can be done." Be it regression or reframing, the acceptance and the work has to be done by the patient. The therapist presents the possibility of wondering or of looking at it as a reframe, but it is always left to the patient to apply these suggestions to her own memory.

***

How good it is to hear Erickson's voice again! And our reliable and steady guide, Ernest Rossi, after more than 15 years of studying and practicing Erickson's approaches, brings us his mature understanding, while allowing us to witness the process by which he came to this understanding. As in his previous books with Erickson, Rossi does not intrude himself between Erickson and the reader. He presents a transcript which allows us to actually witness Erickson at work, in 1945. Then, in his typically modest fashion, he acts as an inquiring student, encouraging Erickson to explain the thinking behind his therapeutic approaches.

He and Erickson also discus many other interesting subjects, including the nature of therapy; human nature, the development of consciousness, and even the evolution and function of slang and obscenity.

Perhaps because Erickson, one year before his death, was ready to explain himself more than he had previously, Rossi was able to get almost direct answers to some of his questions, rather than the colorful and metaphorical responses which Erickson seemed to prefer. Certainly, those metaphorical and "guru-like" answers have stimulated the thinking and growth of hundreds of his students, but we appreciate some simpler, more easily grasped formulations as well. Even Margaret Mead (Mead, 1977) wrote about the pleas which she and other students of Erickson made "for simpler, more repetitious, more boring demonstrations." Rossi, with his patience and persistence, was able to evoke some simpler, clearer explanations to help us understand the essence of Erickson's work.

In this book we can see the amount of work which Erickson put into preparing his patient for changing. Even though it was done in a playful, and sometimes offhand manner—playing games with words, having her write upside down and with both hands at the same time, and getting her to agree "absolutely" in advance, that she would be cured—it is apparent that he felt that this preparation was essential. At the same time, he was fine-tuning the therapeutic relationship, maintaining a challenging and yet trusting tone. As Rossi points out, he was mostly concerned with encouraging and stimulating the processes which will enable the patient to change. Insight seeking was only one of these processes, perhaps one of the least important. When we observe Erickson guiding his patient towards insights and connections with the past, we may, indeed, speculate that this was done largely in response to her conviction that understanding of the past would be necessary before she could be cured.

Erickson would say to us, "It is the patient who does the work. All that the therapist does is to provide conditions in which this work can be done." Erickson worked thoroughly and carefully to provide the necessary conditions. He explored and utilized all conceivable elements in communication and education in order to do so. He emphasized, for example, the importance of utilizing the evocative powers and the multiple meanings of words—the patient's and his own. A beautiful example of his respect for words is seen when he notices, in the patient's automatic writing, that she has written a word which can be read as either "living," "giving" or "diving." He uses this observation as a basis for organizing the therapy around the patient's swimming phobia ("diving"), with the belief that, when this phobia is overcome, she will also be freer in "living" and "giving" and will be relieved of her depression. Some readers may feel that he was arbitrary about the interpretation of this one word or of others. In fact, Rossi, himself, accuses him at one point of making "inferences." But we cannot help but be impressed by his painstaking attention to every expression of the patient, as well as to each of his own communications.

We witness, in addition to his deft and careful use of words, many forms of indirect suggestion—phrasing suggestions as questions, for example. While doing this "manipulating," he was constantly asking the patient for permission to intervene and was always ready to change his interventions in response to the patient's reactions. Thus, he demonstrated the respect which was the hallmark of his way of dealing with patients. In fact, we must comment at this point that, although much of the writing about "Ericksonian techniques" emphasizes the brilliance and ingenuity of the therapist, when we observe Erickson, himself, at work, we are impressed more by the presence and the unique creativity of his patients.

What is the value of utilizing regression as the dominant feature in this therapy? While I was reading this book, it became clear to me why Erickson tended to treat almost everyone like a child! I suddenly understood why, at least in his later years, he seemed to be so enamored of corny jokes, childish puzzles and games. I now feel that he understood, probably from having learned it from working with adult patients in the hypnotically regressed state that it is precisely in this "child state" that we are most open to learning, most curious, and most able to change. In order to intensify the patient's experience of regression, Erickson worked consistently to create a remarkably convincing illusion that he really was an older person talking to a young child. He had the "child" reenact and abreact to traumatic experiences and, through discussions, guided her through a reeducation process. As a result, the child had new experiences to add to her memories—positive experiences with a caring and understanding adult. These corrective regression experiences as I have called them exerted a long-lasting effect on the patient even after she returned to her "adult self."

Among the reeducation experiences which the "child" underwent in her discussions with "The February Man" (Erickson "visited" her, in hypnotic age regression for "several years" in February) were some which have become known as "reframing." There are some beautiful examples of reframing in this book. For example, the patient had been feeling guilty over death wishes towards her younger sister and had blamed herself for the sister's near drowning experience Erickson's "reframe" of this led to his saying to her, "All of these years you have been condemning yourself, have you not? ... Why? Perhaps so that you could reach a still better and larger understanding of yourself" (self-condemnation is reframed as a step toward self-understanding). Sibling rivalry is reframed as follows: "Being jealous of Helen when you were a little baby had one meaning. Now, when you are grown up, it has another meaning entirely. Wouldn't you want a little baby to appreciate its own worth, its own personality and its own needs enough to defend them in any way it understood?"

At one point, Rossi suggests to Erickson that the basis of his hypnotic therapy is "abreaction and a restructuring of the patient's mental processes." Erickson corrects him, saying, "It is not restructuring. You give them a more complete view." Rossi is then able to sum up his understanding with the comment, "it [hypnotic therapy] simply facilitates a more complete, comprehensive point of view and frees one from the limitations and literalism of childhood." This is a far cry from the belief of many therapists that hypnosis involves some kind of reprogramming.

In the treatment of this case we see the beginning of an approach which Jay Haley was to call, "prescribing the symptom." When the patient was apparently ready to try to swim, Erickson forbade her from doing so. He explains, "I place my inhibition on her swimming." After doing this, he points out, "I can change mine!" And, of course, he withdrew his inhibition at the time of his next session with her.

Erickson also gives an interesting rationale for having other people present during therapy:

> This fear, this anxiety about swimming, is observed in relation to other people.... You need to get over some of these fears and anxieties that are manifested in relationship to other people and concealed from other people ... by bringing them out so that it can be realized that one can live even if others do know. We like people best when we know that they are real in a lot of little things.

Group therapists have known these for a long time. But we must remember that group therapy was not much used in 1945.

I admit that, like many others, when I first read the "February Man" case as it is presented in the books, *Hypnotherapy* (Erickson & Rossi, 1979) and *Uncommon Therapy* (Haley, 1973), I was excited by the idea that this appeared to be the first instance in which a therapist had actually changed the history of a patient. I now understand that this change, like many other changes in therapy, actually consists of "widening the frame," or expanding awareness, in the present, not in the past. In fact, I remember Erickson's frequent comment that "understanding the past will not change the past" The "reality" of age regression has been, justifiably, questioned. I believe that, in addition to an "opening up" to actual memories, a large element of fantasy is frequently involved. But regression does not need to be "real" in order to be helpful. Simply, the subjective feeling of being young may make it possible for a patient to view matters from different perspectives. It may also intensify the therapist-patient contact and lead to therapeutic abreactions.

Before terminating the therapy, Erickson helped the patient to ventilate hostility towards him. He reasons that this is important because patients often are angry at the therapist for taking away their symptoms and may express their anger by destroying their therapeutic work. Here, again, he shows exquisite concern for maintaining all therapeutic gains.

The time is approaching when we will see more critical reviews of Erickson and his work. Even those of us who were "hypnotized" by him will evaluate our experiences differently with the passage of time. At this point, however. When I think of him, it is with love—even though he was not a particularly "loving" person, in the usual sense of the word. He conveyed his love and his respect, for me and for countless others by "telling it like it is." For example, once, when I told him that I wanted to be able to experience rather than to intellectualize, he responded, "Your behavior indicates otherwise. You prefer to understand rather than to experience." Typically, he followed this incisive comment with the suggestion, "but you can intellectualize in different ways." Finally, he led me, in trance, into an experience which combined thinking and feeling. He began with a hypnotic induction which started with "In my way of living I often like to climb a mountain—and I always wonder what's on the other side." Thus, he role modelled a different way of intellectualizing by wondering. And it is only now, eight years later while writing this foreword, that I realized that he had done that!

For those of us who have worked with Erickson, there is always much more to learn from him as we peruse and study his work especially the verbatim accounts of his work and thinking as presented here. For the vast majority of readers, for whom this may be the first or second book they have read about Erickson, it will prove well worth-while to read it either quickly or slowly. If read quickly, it will lead to an appreciation of why so much interest has been devoted recently to Erickson. If studied slowly it will stimulate ideas which will enrich the work of any therapist. Thank you, Ernest Rossi, for bringing us this gift.

Note

1 This chapter was previously published in *The February Man: Evolving Consciousness and Identity in Hypnotherapy*, 1989 by Milton H. Erickson and Ernest Rossi, as the Foreword.

References

Erickson, M.H., and Rossi, E. (1979). *Hypnotherapy: An Exploratory Casebook*. New York: Irvington.

Haley, J. (1973). *Uncommon Therapy: The Psychiatric Techniques of Milton H. Erickson, M.D.* New York: W.W. Norton & Co., Inc.

Mead, M. (1977). The Originality of Milton Erickson. *American Journal of Clinical Hypnosis*, 20(1): 4–5.

11

HYPNOTHERAPY: AN EXPLORATORY CASEBOOK FOREWORD[1]

Introduction

I was always struck that Erickson chose me to present his theories. I had done some experimenting with hypnosis, and Ernest Rossi had, too, but we had not spelled out our ideas in theoretical form. Erickson selected us knowing that neither Rossi nor I had any strong theoretical suggestions about how hypnosis worked. And Erickson, too, was atheoretical. He dealt with material that comes up and encouraged the emergence of the material but didn't try to put it into a theoretical package.

Systematizing his approach was made even more difficult because of a quality that Margaret Mead emphasized on his seventy-fifth birthday: his originality. Mead said Erickson never solved a problem in an old way if he could think of a new way. Like all of his students, I was unable to systematize what Erickson said or wrote. Instead, I found it most helpful to elucidate his approach by allowing him to tell stories, which is why our jointly authored book was called *My Voice Will Go With You*. Erickson's primary way of communicating was by telling stories, rather than by resorting to abstract theories. Erickson believed that abstract theories were a way of limiting people, putting them in boxes, and inhibiting the material that emerged in therapy. If the therapy that we talk about has to fit into a theory, it limits the material that can come out.

What's essential for cure is re-association and reorganization of ideas and understanding. Erickson believed that direct suggestions weren't the best way of doing that. Direct suggestion tends to evoke a direct response, not an open invitation. Instead, he believed the therapist's role was to stimulate the patient into activity, often not knowing what that activity may be. Therapy is like starting a snowball rolling down a mountain; it can start an avalanche. You start the snowball rolling; you don't tell it how or where it's going to roll.

Erickson always works toward goals—those of his patients, not his own. We can't say what his goals are until we know what the patients' goals are. He is insisting that we pay attention to the patient's goals. So essentially, he's always trying to help the patient to clarify and address his or her own goals. Of course, Erickson's own values—his emphasis on growth, delight and joy—are present and do affect what comes out. He also insisted on enjoying the process of waiting and becoming what you are. The therapist shouldn't try to impose a predetermined goal but should be open to the goals that emerge from the patient's own associations and growth. That's why Erickson said it's delightful to plant flower seeds and not to know what seeds will come up.

Therapists have questioned whether using deeper trances give more meaningful change. In my experience, deeper trances can involve deeper results involving time distortion and age regression. Like Erickson, I have worked with patients not only in deep trances but in light trances, which Erickson called the common every day trance.

He valued the wisdom of the unconscious and often tried to prevent patients' conscious minds from distracting attention from what the unconscious learnings produced in therapy.

One of these pleasant methods involved his interrupting of what was going on at the end of a session by saying he would like to show the patient some of the Betty Erickson's jewelry, things that he bought from the Phoenix museum. His goal was to avoid the examining of material that emerged from the patient in the trance. He didn't want the patient to look at whatever came out in a trance because if you looked at it, that might undo or destroy what came out. The conscious mind can start questioning what it's come up with and depotentiate the meaningful nexus of the associations.

The approaches discussed in this chapter include the utilization approach, the therapeutic double bind approach, indirect posthypnotic suggestions, and building up compound suggestions.

The utilization approach is to utilize whatever the patient brings in. There's the case where the patient has a delusion, Erickson doesn't try to remove the delusion; instead he tries to utilize it as an example of something the patient is able to do. Or the person who is paranoid and hearing voices telling him that he has to do something or other, like defend himself, and people are trying to kill him. Instead of trying to make the voices go away, which might be a goal with medication, we would utilize those forces and say, "Yes and you do need to consider the directive of the voices and accept them as your own voice, and then decide how to deal with the suggestions." It would be up to him to question the directive to kill himself and come up with another alternative. He might come up with the idea that he doesn't have to kill himself but kill some destructive urges in himself, ignore them, or pass them off as an inner battle.

Given the fact that Erickson was atheoretical, and there is no easily codified guide to his methods, I would suggest the following to therapists who want to use his techniques today. This advice would be to stop trying to imitate him or even see what his techniques are. Instead, therapists should use their own free associations and ideas and share them with their patients. Don't try to emulate Erickson's techniques; follow your curiosity instead of trying to achieve a predetermined goal. See where your curiosity leads.

***

Speak to the wall so the door may hear

Sufi saying

Everyone who knows Milton Erickson is aware that he rarely does anything without a purpose. In fact, his goal-directedness may be the most important characteristic of his life and work.

Why is it, then, that prior to writing *Hypnotic Realities* with Ernest Rossi (Erickson & Rossi, 1976) he had avoided presenting his work in book form? Why did he choose Ernest Rossi to coauthor that book and the present one? And, finally, I could not help but wonder, why did he ask me to write this foreword?

Erickson has, after all, published almost 150 articles over a 50-year period, but only two relatively minor books—*Time Distortion in Hypnosis*, written in 1954 with L.S. Cooper (Erickson 1954), and *The Practical Applications of Medical and Dental Hypnosis*, in 1961 with S. Hershman, M.D. and I.I. Sector, DDS (Erickson 1961). It is easy to understand that in his seventies he may well be eager to leave a legacy, a definitive summing up, a final opportunity for others to really understand and perhaps emulate him.

Rossi is an excellent choice as a coauthor. He is an experienced clinician who has trained with many giants in psychiatry—Franz Alexander, amongst others. He is a Jungian training analyst. He is a prolific author and has devoted the major part of his time over the past six years to painstaking observation, recording and discussion of Erickson's work.

Again, why me? I am also a training analyst, but with a different group—the American Institute of Psychoanalysis (Karen Horney). I have been a practicing psychiatrist for almost 30 years. For almost 15 years I have also done a great deal of work with disabled patients. I have been involved with hypnosis for over 35 years, since I first heard about Milton Erickson, who was then living in Eloise, Michigan.

Both Rossi and I have broad, but differing, clinical and theoretical backgrounds. Neither of us has worked primarily with hypnosis. Therefore, neither of us has a vested interest in promoting some hypnotic theories of our own. We are genuinely devoted to the goal of presenting Erickson's theories and ideas, not only to practitioners of hypnosis, but to the community of psychotherapists and psychoanalysts which has had little familiarity with hypnosis. Towards this end, Rossi assumes the posture of a rather naive student acting on behalf of the rest of us.

Margaret Mead, who also counts herself as one of his students, writes of the originality of Milton Erickson in the issue of *The American Journal of Clinical Hypnosis* dedicated to him on his seventy-fifth birthday (Mead, 1977). She comments that she has been interested in his originality ever since she first met him in the summer of 1940, expanding on this idea by stating it can be firmly said that Milton Erickson never solved a problem in an old way if he can think of a new way—and he usually can. She feels, however, that his unquenchable, burning originality was a barrier to the transmission of much of what he knew and that inquiring students would become bemused with the extraordinary and unexpected quality of each different demonstration, lost between trying to imitate the intricate, idiosyncratic response and the underlying principles which he was illuminating. In *Hypnotic Realities* and in this book, Ernest Rossi takes some large steps towards elucidating these underlying principles. He does this most directly by organizing and extracting them from Erickson's case material. Even more helpfully, though, he encourages Erickson to spell out some of these principles.

Students who study this volume carefully, as I did, will find that the authors have done the best job to date in clarifying Erickson's ideas on the nature of hypnosis and hypnotic therapy, on techniques of hypnotic induction, on ways of inducing therapeutic change, and of validating this change. In the process they have also revealed a great deal of helpful data about Erickson's philosophy of life and therapy. Many therapists, both psychoanalytic and others, will find his approaches compatible with their own and far removed from their preconceptions about hypnosis. As the authors point out, Hypnosis does not change the person nor does it alter past experiential life. It serves to permit him to learn more about himself and to express himself more adequately.... Therapeutic trance helps people side-step their own learned limitations so that they can more fully explore and utilize their potentials.

Those who read Erickson's generous offering of fascinating case histories, and then attempt to emulate him, will undoubtedly find that they do not achieve results that are at all comparable to his. They may then give up, deciding that Erickson's approach is one that is unique for him. They may note that Erickson has several handicaps that have always set him apart from others, and that may certainly permit him to have a unique way of viewing and responding. He was born with color deficient vision, tone deafness, dyslexia, and lacking a sense of rhythm. He suffered two serious attacks of crippling poliomyelitis. He has been wheelchair bound for many years from the effects of the neurological damage, supplemented by arthritis and myositis. Some will not be content with the rationalization that Erickson is a therapeutic or inimitable genius. And they will find that with the help of clarifiers and facilitators, such as Ernest Rossi, there is much in his way of working that can be learned, taught and utilized by others.

Erickson himself has advised, in *Hypnotic Realities* (Erickson & Rossi, 1976, p. 258), in working at a problem of difficulty, you try to make an interesting design in the handling of it. That way you have an answer to the difficult problem.

Become interested in the design and don't notice the back-breaking labor. In dealing with the difficult problem of analyzing and teaching Erickson's approaches, Rossi's designs can be most helpful. Whether each reader will choose to accept Rossi's suggestion that he practice the exercises recommended in this book, is an individual matter; in my experience, it has been worthwhile to practice some of them. In fact, by deliberately and planfully applying some of Erickson's approaches as underlined by Rossi, I found that I have been able to help patients experience deeper states of trance and be more open to changing as an apparent consequence of this. I found that setting up therapeutic double binds, giving indirect posthypnotic suggestions, using questions to facilitate therapeutic responsiveness, and building up compound suggestions have been particularly helpful. Erickson and Rossi's repeated emphasis on what they call the utilization approach is certainly justified. In this book they give many vivid and useful examples of accepting and utilizing the patient's manifest behavior, utilizing the patient's inner realities, utilizing the patient's resistances, and utilizing the patient's negative affect and symptoms. Erickson's creative use of jokes, puns, metaphors and symbols has been analyzed by others, notably Haley and Bandler and Grinder, but the examples and discussion in this book add a great deal to our understanding.

At times, Erickson will work with a patient in a light trance, in what he calls a common everyday trance, or no trance at all. He does not limit himself to short-term therapy. This is illustrated in his painstaking work over a nine-month period with Pietro, the flutist with the swollen lip, described in one of the dramatic case outlines in this book. His expertise, however, in working with patients in the deepest trances, often with amnesia for the therapeutic work, has always interested observers. The question of whether or not inducing deeper trances, and giving directions or suggestions indirectly rather than directly, leads to more profound or lasting clinical results is a researchable one. It has certainly been my experience that if one does not believe in, or value, deeper trances and does not strive for them, one is not likely to see them very often. My experience has also been that the achievement of deeper trances, often including phenomena such as dissociation, time distortion, amnesia, and age-regression, does lead to quicker and apparently more profound changes in patients' symptoms and attitudes.

Erickson emphasizes the value of helping patients to work in the mode of what he would call the unconscious. He values the wisdom of the unconscious. In fact, he often goes to great lengths to keep the therapeutic work from being examined and potentially destroyed by the patient's conscious mind and by the patient's learned and limited sets. His methods of doing this are more explicitly outlined in this book than in any other writings available to date.

It is true that he tends not to distinguish between induction of trance or hypnotic techniques and therapeutic techniques or maneuvers. He feels that it is a waste of time for the therapist to use meaningless, repetitious phrases in the induction of trance as this time might be more usefully employed injecting therapeutic suggestions or in preparing the patient for change. As Rossi has pointed out, both the therapy and trance, induction involves, in the early stages, a depotentiation of the patient's usual and limited mental sets. Erickson is never content with simply inducing a trance, but is always concerned with some therapeutic role.

He points out the limited effectiveness of direct suggestion, although he is certainly aware that hypnotic techniques, using direct suggestion, will frequently enhance the effectiveness of behavior modification approaches such as desensitization and cognitive retraining. He notes that direct suggestion does not evoke the re-association and reorganization of ideas, understandings and memories so essential for an actual cure. Effective results in hypnotic psychotherapy derive only from the patient's activities. The therapist merely stimulates the patient into activity, often not knowing what that activity may be. And then he guides the patient and exercises clinical judgment in determining the amount of work to be done to achieve the desired results (Erickson, 1948). From this comment, and from reading the case histories in this volume and in other publications, it should be apparent that Erickson demands and evokes much less doctrinal compliance than do most therapists.

It is obvious that clinical judgment comes only as the result of many years of intensive study of dynamics, pathology and health, and from actually working with patients.

The judgment of the therapist will also be influenced by his own philosophy and goals in life. Erickson's own philosophy is manifested by his emphasis on concepts such as growth and delight and joy. To this he adds, "Life isn't something you can give an answer to today. You should enjoy the process of waiting, the process of becoming what you are. There is nothing more delightful than planting flower seeds and not knowing what kinds of flowers are going to come up." My own experience in this regard is illustrated by my having visited him in 1970, spending a four-hour session with him, and leaving with the feeling that I had spent this time mostly in listening to stories about his family and patients. I did not see him again until the summer of 1977. Then, at 5:00 A.M. in a Phoenix motel, while I was reviewing some tapes of Erickson at work, some very important insights became vividly evident to me. They were obviously related to work begun during our session in 1970 and to self-analysis I had done in the intervening seven years. Later that morning when I excitedly mentioned these insights to Erickson, he, typically, simply smiled and did not attempt to elaborate on them in any way.

When we read some of the writings on other forms of therapy, such as family therapy or Gestalt therapy, we are struck by how much they have been influenced by Erickson. This is no accident as many of the early therapists in these schools began working with hypnosis or even with Erickson himself. I hope that Rossi will trace some of these influences in his future writings. I have alluded to some of them in my article, "Recent Experiences with Encounter Gestalt and Hypnotic Techniques" (Rosen, 1972).

In conjunction with Erickson and Rossi's first volume Hypnotic Realities, Hypnotherapy: An Exploratory Casebook should serve as a firm basis for courses in Ericksonian therapy or Ericksonian hypnosis. These courses may be supplemented by other books, including those written by J. Haley and by Bandler and Grinder. In addition, we are now fortunate to have available a bibliography of the 147 articles written by Erickson himself (Gravitz, & Gravitz,1977).

Rossi has told me that in working with Erickson he has always been struck by the fact that Erickson seems to be atheoretical. I have noted that this applies to Erickson's openness but certainly not to his emphasis on growth or his humanistic or socially oriented views. Rossi and others are constantly rediscovering the fact that Erickson always works towards goals—those of his patients', not his own. This may not seem to be such a revolutionary idea today when it is the avowed intention of almost all therapists, but perhaps many of us are limited in our capacity to carry out this intent. It is significant that both intent and practice are most successfully coordinated and realized in the work of this man who is probably the world's master in clinical hypnosis, and yet hypnosis is still associated by almost everyone with manipulation and suggestion—a typical Ericksonian paradox. The master manipulator allows and stimulates the greatest freedom!

Note

1 This chapter was previously published in *Hypnotherapy: An Exploratory Casebook*, 1979 by Milton H. Erickson and Ernest Rossi, as the Foreword.

References

Erickson, M.H., and Cooper, L.S. (1954). *Time Distortion in Hypnosis*. Baltimore: Williams & Wilkins.
Erickson, M.H., and Rossi, E. (1976). *Hypnotic Realities*. New York: Irvington.
Erickson, M.H., and Rossi, E. (1979). *Hypnotherapy: An Exploratory Casebook*. New York: Irvington.
Erickson, M.H., Hershman, S., and Sector, I.I. (1961). *The Practical Applications of Medical and Dental Hypnosis*. New York: Brunner/Mazel.
Gravitz, M.A., and Gravitz, R.F. (1977). The Collected Writings of Milton H. Erickson: Complete Bibliography 1929–1977. *American Journal of Clinical Hypnosis*, 20(1): 84–94.
Haley, J. (1973). *Uncommon Therapy: The Psychiatric Techniques of Milton H. Erickson, M.D.* New York: W.W. Norton & Co., Inc.
Mead, M. (1977). The Originality of Milton Erickson. *American Journal of Clinical Hypnosis*, 20(1): 4–5.
Rosen, S. (1972). Recent Experiences with Encounter, Gestalt, And Hypnotic Techniques. *American Journal of Psychoanalysis*, 32(1): 90–102.

12

STORIES FOR THE THIRD EAR FOREWORD[1]

Introduction

In 1982, I published with Erickson, *My Voice Will Go with You: The Teaching Tales of Milton Erickson*. Attending sessions with Erickson up until 1980, I became convinced that his best way of teaching was through what I called his teaching tales. Some of the most effective interventions which Erickson demonstrated at this time were through these teaching tales. A teaching tale is like a biblical narrative, a tale that serves a purpose of teaching. Erickson included in his teaching tales his work with patients as well as with his family and professional colleagues. In these tales he modeled and role modeled the patient's experience. In other words, many of the stories illustrate his interventions and observations by giving examples of what he meant by the central elements of therapy: "First you model the patient's world, then you role model the patient's world."

To spell out what I mean by modeling and role modeling: we model a person's behavior, repeating his behavior, speaking in a certain tone of voice, leaning forward with our shoulders—that would be modeling a person's behavior. Modeling a person's world involves telling stories that spell out what the patient's world was like. Role modeling a patient's world is presenting someone else's world, and their way of looking at it.

For example, we can model a patient's behavior by simply imitating her bodily movements and tones of voice. We can also model the world by feeding back to the patient observations about the patient's world. These observations may have been conveyed to us by the patients describing his or her troubles, conflicts, and symptoms. If a patient were to say, "I can't make sense of my life," that complaint could be modeled by the therapist by saying, "You can't make sense of your life." That would model the world. To role model that patient's world might be a way in which symptoms and responses are spelled out in a form that makes sense. For example, I would tell a story in which someone has been able to make sense of their life. So, the modeling involves summarizing the symptoms and problems and disputations of the patient's life and the role modeling involves presenting someone else, or Erickson himself, in the same situation, having made sense of it. It's a story in which sense somehow emerges.

I felt that his most effective way of teaching was through the telling of these teaching tales. So, in the book I used transcripts of tapes that I made of his teaching with me and other therapists and I included own commentary on their meaning. The book was received as Erickson's way of guiding readers and making interventions. I'm impressed by the similarity between his teaching tales and Biblical stories, other inspiring stories or parables of learning.

Lee Wallas' stories also function as teaching tales. As her book "Stories for the Third Ear" makes clear, these tales need not be in the form of fairy tales. They could just as easily evolve around science. They show that Erickson inspired Lee Wallas to come up with teaching tales of her own, just as her teaching tales inspired other therapists to produce their own teaching tales, from science fiction to poetry. She helped therapists guide patients into what I call "learning trances."

***

Milton H. Erickson, one of the most effective and innovative psychotherapists of our time, died on March 25, 1980. Since that time there has been an outpouring of books attempting to transmit and explain his teachings. Erickson stated that *"the practice of psychotherapy should be interesting, appealing and charming,"* and one of the elements in his therapy, particularly in his later years, was the utilization of what I have called "teaching tales". Lee Wallas calls them "stories for the third ear." These stories not only add an element of charm and beauty to the psychotherapy in which they are used, but there is increasing clinical evidence that their use adds to the effectiveness of therapy.

As interpreters of Milton Erickson have pointed out, and as Erickson himself stated, the central elements in his therapy were, "First you model the patient's world; then you role model the patient's world." Both the modeling and role-modeling can be done in the form of stories. The first part of the story analogues the patient's symptoms, problems or life situation, thereby modeling the patient's world, or part of it. The second part of the story analogues or role-models solutions or optional ways of looking at or dealing with the patient's situation.

The excellent stories presented here by Lee Wallas, who is a creative and experienced therapist, follow this Ericksonian prescription. And, as Erickson said of some of his own talks, the stories "came to her" when she herself was in a trance state. They were presented to patients who were also in a trance state.

Erickson defined hypnosis as "the evocation and utilization of unconscious learnings." He felt that we are in close touch with our own inner knowledge and in best rapport with our patients or clients when both of us are in a "shared" trance. He believed that we are most open to learning in that state. Lee Wallas gives the therapists clear and explicit directions for helping patients to enter and utilize these "learning trances." She also shares with us some of her ways of preparing them to "receive the riches." The Sufis and others felt that this preparation was most important in the imparting of any teaching.

Simply entering into a trance state seems to enable most therapists to tap the poetic elements of their own psyche and it may be that this poetic element is directly connected with emergence of "unconscious" mentation, hopefully of a wise nature. Of course, Wallas does not imply that the mere telling of a tale will cure anyone. She describes many other therapeutic factors (e.g., insisting that an alcoholic patient attend A.A. meetings), often involving months or every years of work. But one cannot help but be impressed by the power of a teaching tale, when it is utilized properly. I have seen and heard of many instances in which patient's behavior has changed positively after a teaching tale has been utilized—either one which was borrowed from Erickson, from the Bible, from folk tales, or one which was created by the therapist.

Experienced therapists will certainly find that studying the composition and use of language in Lee Wallas' stories can inspire them and help them to develop their own "teaching tales." These tales need not be in the form of fairy tales. They could just as easily evolve around science fiction, poetry, other literary forms, even recipes of menus. They might involve the use of music or movement metaphors, as expressed in dance.

Therapists who explore these approaches will be moving in directions which Erickson encouraged—towards the discovery of more effective ways of helping people to "learn to think" and to grow.

Note

1 This chapter was previously published in *Stories for the Third Ear*, 1985, by Lee Wallas, as the Foreword.

INDEX

Abraham, Karl 3
acupuncture 31–32, 35
age progression 20, 79
age regression 20, 100, 101, 125, 126, 129, 132
agoraphobia, story of woman with agoraphobic symptoms 73
air, as concretizing resource 52–53
Alexander, Franz 130
allergist story 1, 3
Allport, Gordon 26
altered states of consciousness: Erickson/Huxley collaboration 13; interpersonally 24; intrapsychically 23–24; and new mental set 67–68
American Institute of Psychoanalysis 130
American Journal of Clinical Hypnosis, Erickson's 75th birthday issue 34
The American Journal of Clinical Hypnosis, issue dedicated to Erickson 131
American Psychoanalytic Association 33, 72
amnesia 49, 132
animal magnetism 63
anthropology: Erickson's contribution to 65; Erickson's stories focused on 117, 119
anxiety: and concretizing of symptoms 48–49, 51, 52; and depotentiation of usual mental sets 24; and explanations/insight 26; and negative switches 39; and physical switches 64; and reframing 17; relief from vs. achieving one's potential 16, 17; and remembering the past 97; and sense of mastery 78; and "start and stop" technique 71; and willpower 32
arm levitation inductions 66, 82
authority 11–12
autobiography, Erickson's views on 9
automatic writing 42, 124
autonomic conditioning 101
autosuggestions 8, 26–27, 73, 101
"awakening in a strange hotel room" story (Erickson) 73
Awareness Continuum Exercise (Gestalt therapy) 35, 37

bad luck, Erickson's views on 9
Bandler, Richard 132, 134
Barber, T.X. 100–101, 108
Bateson, Gregory 65
Beahrs, John O. 33–34
becoming, "You should enjoy the process of waiting, the process of becoming what you are" (Erickson) 4, 133
behavioral desensitization 35, 39, 78, 81, 113, 133
behavioral therapies 19, 41, 113, 114
Belo, Jane 65
Benson, Herbert, Relaxation Response 35
Berne, Eric 103, 115
Betz, B.J. 19
Biblical tales 135, 136, 137
bioenergetic analysis 114
Blake, William 5, 38, 48

body language 72
Braid, James 63
breathing: breathing in (concretizing air) 52–53; focus on 35; as switch 64
Bronowski, J. 5, 48
Buber, Martin 24
Bucholtz, Melvyn: Japanese culture, love for shared with Rosen vii; meeting with Erickson vii; meeting with Rosen vii; on Rosen's essays on Erickson viii–x

cancer patients: case of patient with nausea as result of chemotherapy 58–60; concretizing of resources in 53; *see also* Hypnosis as an Adjunct to Chemotherapy in Cancer (Sidney Rosen)
cases *see* patients' stories
Catholicism, statues and religious objects 50
childhood: "child state" 125; "child within" 38, 60; early childhood regression 79, 122; Erickson's views on raising children 10–12; "Every child likes a surprise" (Erickson) 21, 63, 90; limitations/literalism of childhood 126; malleability of childhood viii–ix, 21; and reframing 20; as world of magic viii–ix, 21–22, 92, 96
coenesthesia 8
cognitive retraining 133
cognitive therapies 41
collective unconscious 89
Colorado Psychopathic Hospital, "I'm going to die next Saturday morning" story 27
communication: multilevel communication 21; nonverbal communication 20, 67, 72
compound suggestions 129, 132
Concretizing of Symptoms and Their Manipulation (Sidney Rosen): chapter overview by Kiarsis xii; concretizing of resources 52–53; concretizing of resources in cancer patients 53; concretizing of symbols 47; concretizing of symptoms as part of overall therapy 60; concretizing vs. symbolizing 50–52; imagination and free will 48; literalness and concreteness of hypnotized subjects 49, 60; manipulation of concretized symptom 49, 51–52; patient with abdominal pain 47, 53–54; patient with fear of heights and allergies 47, 56–58; patient with hair-pulling compulsion (trichotillomania) 47, 54–56; patient with nausea as result of chemotherapy 58–60; physical objects 49–50, 52; Sara (ex-nun) 47, 51; woman bedeviled with hallucinations of naked men 48–49; woman seeing "LOVE" broken in two 51
confusion techniques 28, 31, 41, 67, 82
consciousness *see* altered states of consciousness
control, Kay Thompson on 120
conversational inductions 117–118, 120
Cooper, L.S., *Time Distortion in Hypnosis* (Erickson and Cooper) 130
corrective regression 20, 122–123, 125
Cravens, Gwynn 14
Creighton, J.L. 80
crystal healing 32, 35
curiosity 9, 37, 73, 92, 130

Daitzman, Reid J., *Mental Jogging* 46
death 2, 14
deep sleep (as induction technique) 86
Delphi, Oracle of 23
depotentiation of usual mental sets 24, 67, 133
depression 9, 16, 24, 48–49, 51, 52
Deren, Maya 65
desensitization 35, 39, 78, 81, 113, 133
D'Eslon, Charles-Nicolas 38
diagnosing 26
direct suggestion 75, 128, 133
dissociation 20, 31, 36, 95, 132
doing and learning 8–10
double bind approach 129, 132
dreams: to be expressed in present tense (Erickson) 101; Gestalt interpretation techniques 106–107; guided hypnotic dreams (Sacerdote) 100; suggestions for healing dreams (Rosen) 81; "the unexplainable fits into the realm of the spirit" (Erickson on dreams) 2
"Dry Beds" story: "Dry Beds" story as told by Erickson 68–70, 71; Erickson as master manipulator 76; Erickson on awakening in strange hotel room 73; Erickson on direct suggestion and therapist's role 75; Erickson on hypnosis as "evocation and utilization of unconscious learnings" 75; Erickson on "something that you know but don't know that you know" 68, 69; Erickson on therapy being "like a snowball rolling

down a mountain" 75; Ericksonian hypnosis vs. psychoanalytic therapy 75; imagination and suggestion 63–64; inner search 68; interactive nature of hypnosis 72; nonverbal and body language 72; "start and stop" technique 71, 119; story of college freshman wanting to quit school (Rosen) 73–75; story of woman with agoraphobic symptoms (Rosen) 73; story of woman with large gap between front teeth (Erickson) 71; trusting one's unconscious mind 71; waiting technique 68

early learning set inductions xii, 36–38, 45, 88, 95
ego-boosting suggestions 25
ego-syntonic suggestions 36, 72
EMDR (Eye Movement Desensitization and Reprocessing) 35
Emerson, Ralph Waldo, on poetry ix
Encounter therapy: contributions of encounter movement 114; dangers of encounter groups 111; group trance 97; hypnotic experiences 107–108; physical tasks 100; techniques from theater 114, 115
Encyclopedia Britannica, hypnosis section 62
Enright, J.B. 102
Erickson, Allan 13
Erickson, Betty: discussing Erickson's values with 2; on Erickson being a strict disciplinarian 10–11; on Erickson's desire for privacy 6; on Erickson's views on religion 8; on Erickson's views on supernatural/paranormal 8; on Erickson's views on women 12; gift of *Topsys and Turvys* book 45; on her son Allan 13; jewelry 129
Erickson, Kristi 11
Erickson, Lance 14
Erickson, Milton H. (biographical details): death 136; discovery of alphabetic order as a child 66; favorite puzzle 45; friendship with Bucholtz vii; fun with the family 2; International Congress (1980) devoted to his work 64–65, 67; photographs of xvi, xvii; physical handicaps and illness 2, 3, 72, 131; Rosen, hypnosis of 123, 127; Rosen, meetings with 63, 67, 97, 133; Rosen's friends Jack and Art, meeting with 62–63, 67; Rossi and Rosen chosen for presentation of his theories 128, 130; secretaries and typing patterns 7; teaching seminars 25, 42; *see also* Erickson, Milton H. (quotes); Erickson, Milton H. (writings)
Erickson, Milton H. (quotes): on the "African violet queen of Milwaukee" 9; on autobiography 6; "awakening in a strange hotel room" story 73; on bad luck 9; on direct suggestion and therapist's role 75; on "disciplining of two-and-a-half year old Kristi" 11; "Don't hold on to hurt feelings" 40; "Enjoy your life" 8–9; "Every child likes a surprise" 21, 63, 90; "First you model the patient's world, and then you role model the patient's world" 16, 20, 42, 67, 135, 136; on giving patients "a more complete view" 125–126; on group therapy 126; "Hypnosis is the evocation and utilization of unconscious learnings" 16, 20, 23, 27, 33, 66, 75, 136; on hypnotic regression to infancy/womb 7; "I don't believe in salvation only through pain and suffering" 9; "I have human curiosity working for me" 9; "I know how to speak" 44; "I know my own voice" 87; "I know that I can never really understand the language of another person" 20; "I like to climb a mountain" 5, 63, 127; "I think that is entirely premature. I have no intention of dying" 2, 14; on indirect suggestions 28; "It is the patient who does the work" ix, 123, 124; "It's just that people are so expressive" 7; "It's painful, but if you consider the alternatives, you prefer to experience the pain" 2; on maladies and therapeutic disruption of pattern 80; on manipulation 10; "many of the things we now do automatically" 36, 41, 45; on memory 6; "most of your life is unconsciously determined" 45; "new theory for each patient" 19; on parapsychology 7; "the practice of psychotherapy should be interesting, appealing and charming" 136; on protecting the patient 5–6; on "roughage of life" 93; "Spread humor knee deep everywhere" 28; on supernatural phenomena 7–8; "Therapy cannot be learned from books. It is

learned from life/experience" 5, 25, 43; "Therapy is like a snowball rolling down a mountain" 23, 75, 128; "Therapy is the substitution of a good idea for a bad idea" xii, 21, 32, 38; "There is something that you know but don't know that you know" 22, 68, 69; on thinking 43; "understanding the past will not change the past" 126; "the unexplainable fits into the realm of the spirit" (dreams) 2; "We all have our limitations" 28; "We learn our goals only in the process of getting there" 4; on welfare aid 9–10; "Why do patients do the crazy things [I] ask?" 27–28; "You know much more than you think you know" 6, 22; "You should enjoy the process of waiting, the process of becoming what you are" 4, 133; "Your unconscious mind will protect your conscious mind" 22; *see also* Erickson, Milton H. (biographical details); Erickson, Milton H. (writings)
Erickson, Milton H. (writings): articles by (number and bibliography) 130, 134; *Hypnotherapy: An Exploratory Casebook* (Erickson and Rossi) 31, 41, 67, 123–124, 125–126, 127, 130; *Hypnotic Realities* (Erickson and Rossi) 130, 131–132, 134; "Learning to Stand Up" 72; *My Voice Will Go with You: The Teaching Tales of Milton H. Erickson, M. D.* (Erickson and Rosen) xi, xii, xiii, 6, 67, 128, 135, 136; *The Practical Applications of Medical and Dental Hypnosis* (Erickson, Hershman, and Sector) 130; *Time Distortion in Hypnosis* (Erickson and Cooper) 130; *see also* Erickson, Milton H. (biographical details); Erickson, Milton H. (quotes)
Erickson, Robert 11
Erickson International Congress (1980) 64–65, 67
Erikson, Erik 64
ESP (extrasensory perception) 7–8
esthetics 13; *see also* poetry
The Evocative Power of Language (Sidney Rosen): chapter overview by Kiarsis xiii; commentary on Kay Thompson's approach 117; commonality and differences between Erickson's and Thompson's approaches 117, 119; control (Kay Thomson on) 120;
conversational inductions 117–118, 120; directives for reinforcement 119; "I believe that everything that I say is leading toward the ultimate goal" (Thompson) 118; injunctive approach 118–119; intense interpersonal trances 118; interspersed suggestions 117–118, 120; metaphors 117, 119; "Not a word passes my lips before I have thought of it first" (Thompson) 118; pain transferred to clenched fist 117, 119; poetic language 119; post-hypnotic suggestions 117, 119, 120; reframing 117, 119; "therapizing/teaching trance" (Rosen) 120; time distortion technique 118, 120; from trance to trance 120; word play 117, 118, 119, 120
existential psychology 101, 109, 112, 113
experiencing 5, 25–26, 43, 65, 97–98, 109
explanations, vs. pseudo-explanations 26
externalizations 103–104
extrasensory perception (ESP) 7–8
Eye Movement Desensitization and Reprocessing (EMDR) 35

fairy tales 136, 137
family stories, Erickson's focus on 117, 119
family therapy, Erickson's contribution to 64–65, 133
fear of height, case of patient with fear of heights and allergies 47, 56–58
The February Man Foreword (Sidney Rosen): chapter overview by Kiarsis xiii; corrective regression 20, 122–123, 125; helping patient to ventilate anger towards therapist 126; hypnotherapy as "giving patient a more complete view" (Erickson) 125–126; "I like to climb a mountain" (Erickson) 127; indirect suggestions 125; insight, minor role of 124; "It is the patient who does the work" (Erickson) ix, 123, 124; patient with fear of swimming and self-condemnation 122, 123, 124, 125, 126; "prescribing the symptom" (Jay Haley) 126; rationale for group therapy (Erickson) 126; reframing 122, 123, 125; Rosen hypnotized by Erickson (tendency to intellectualize) 123, 127; Rossi's work with Erickson (*Hypnotherapy: An Exploratory Casebook*) 123–124, 125–126, 127; "understanding the past will not change the past" (Erickson) 126

flexibility (of therapeutic approaches) 20
folk tales 137
Frank, J. 19, 24, 25
Frankl, Viktor 104, 113
free association 27, 36, 43, 89, 130
free will 48
Freud, Sigmund: personality types 3; suggestion 26; superego 103; theory of the unconscious 89; *see also* neo-Freudians; psychoanalysis/psychoanalytic therapies
Fromm, Erich 3
Fromm-Reichmann, Frieda 25
Frost, Robert vii

genetic and racial differences, Erickson's views on 12–13
Gestalt therapy: Awareness Continuum Exercise 35, 37; "completing the Gestalt" 111; dream interpretation 106–107; Erickson's influence on 133; experiencing 109; externalizations 103–104; focus on one thing 32; group trance 97; "hot seat" technique 102–103; humanistic psychology therapeutic school 113–114; hypnotic experiences 107–108; main principles 102; patient's responsibility for himself 109; physical encounters (Louise case) 104–105; presentness 101, 102; techniques 98; therapist-patient relationship 24; "top dog" - "underdog" inner dialogue 103
Ginsburg, Allen vii
goals: patient's goals 129, 134; therapist's goals 16, 28; "We learn our goals only in the process of getting there" (Erickson) 4; *see also* Hypnosis as an Adjunct to Chemotherapy in Cancer (Sidney Rosen)
Goethe, Johann Wolfgang von, on limitations 1
Goodman, Paul 113
Grinder, John 132, 134
group hypnotic induction *see* A Guided Fantasy (Sidney Rosen)
group therapy 98–99, 104–105, 113, 126
group trance 88, 97
A Guided Fantasy (Sidney Rosen): chapter overview by Kiarsis xiii; early learning set induction 88, 95; "Every child likes a surprise" (Erickson) 90; group hypnotic induction 88; group hypnotic induction, participant's comments on 95–96; group

hypnotic induction, transcript of 90–95; "I like to climb a mountain" (Erickson and Rosen) 89, 91–92, 95; images and new learnings 89–90; poetry in hypnotic inductions 88–89; unconscious, Erickson's, Freud's and Jung's views of 89; unconscious mind and trance state 88, 90–91
gurus 17–18, 21, 28, 64, 124

Hain, George 17
hair-pulling compulsion (trichotillomania), case of patient with 47, 54–56
Haley, Jay: family therapy 64–65; "prescribing the symptom" 126; *Uncommon Therapy: The Psychiatric Techniques of Milton H. Erickson, M.D.* 4, 9, 66, 71, 126, 132, 134
Hall, H.R. 80
hallucinations, case of woman with hallucinations of naked men 48–49
Hammond, D.C. 28
healers 17–18, 28, 32, 68; *see also* shamans
Hefferline, Ralph 113
height, fear of *see* fear of height
Hershman, S., *The Practical Applications of Medical and Dental Hypnosis* (Erickson, Hershman, and Sector) 130
heterosuggestions 26, 27–28, 101
Hilgard, E.R. 34
Horney, Karen: "All we have to do to do analysis is be with the patient" 66–67; American Institute of Psychoanalysis 130; compulsivity of neurotic patterns 67; curing vs. perfecting neurosis in therapy 16; differences with Erickson's approach 75; externalizations 103–104; family dynamics 75; "Here and Now, the What and How" 101; holistic theory of psychoanalysis 112; insight vs. change 66; "A Morality of Evolution" 109; no differentiation between "treatment" and other contacts with patient 66; personality types 3; "shoulds" 103, 112
"hot seat" technique 102–103
Houdini, Harry 7
humanistic psychology 113–114
Humiston, K.E. 34
humor 2, 14, 16, 28–29
"hurt feelings state" 40–41
Huxley, Aldous, work with Erickson on altered states of consciousness 13
hypersuggestibility 33, 73

hypnoanalysis 20, 100
hypnos (sleep) 63
hypnosis: experiments on nature of 100–101; history of 63; "Hypnosis is the evocation and utilization of unconscious learnings" (Erickson) 16, 20, 23, 27, 33, 66, 75, 136; innovative hypnotic techniques 100; as interactive therapy 72; origin of word 63; vs. parapsychology 7; used in different therapeutic schools 114; as way of learning about oneself ix, 21, 22–23; as way of thinking 46; *see also* Hypnosis as an Adjunct to Chemotherapy in Cancer (Sidney Rosen); induction techniques; One Thousand Induction Techniques and Their Application to Therapy and Thinking (Sidney Rosen); self-hypnosis; suggestions; trance state
Hypnosis as an Adjunct to Chemotherapy in Cancer (Sidney Rosen): chapter overview by Kiarsis xii; deep sleep 86; Erickson on maladies and therapeutic disruption of patterns 80; goal of giving patient sense of mastery 77, 78, 80; goal of minimizing side effects 77, 78, 80, 86; goal of opening unconscious learnings 77; hypnotic induction (example of woman having undergone mastectomy) 82–85; hypnotic intervention vs. marijuana 78; indirect and counter suggestions 81; indirect and metaphorical suggestions 81; projection into future (example of woman with breast cancer) 78–80; self-hypnosis 78, 80, 81, 85; sleep-promoting/healing dreams suggestions on audiotapes 81; sympathetic identification and treating personnel 86–87; time distortion technique 80–81, 82, 86; using patients' values to change their attitudes 81–82
Hypnotherapy: An Exploratory Casebook Foreword (Sidney Rosen): chapter overview by Kiarsis xiii; compatibility between Erickson's approach and other therapies ix–x, 131; compound suggestions 129, 132; deeper trances/deeper results 129, 132; direct suggestions 128, 133; Erickson as master manipulator 134; Erickson's atheoretical approach 128, 129–130, 134; Erickson's choice of Rossi and Rosen to present his theories 128, 130; Erickson's influence on family and Gestalt therapies 133; growth, delight and joy 129, 133; *Hypnotic Realities* (Erickson and Rossi) 130, 131–132, 134; indirect post-hypnotic suggestions 129, 132; Margaret Mead on Erickson's originality 128, 131; patients' goals 129, 134; storytelling 128; therapeutic double bind approach 129, 132; "Therapy is like a snowball rolling down a mountain" (Erickson) 128; unconscious, wisdom of 132; unconscious learnings 129; utilization approach 129, 132; works for Ericksonian therapy courses 134; "You should enjoy the process of waiting, the process of becoming what you are" (Erickson) 133
hypnotics 23–24

imagination (images) 5, 32, 38, 48, 63–64, 89–90, 101
indirect suggestions 28, 31, 65, 73, 81, 125; indirect post-hypnotic suggestions 129, 132
individual, uniqueness of 1, 3
induction techniques: arm levitation inductions 66, 82; conversational inductions 117–118, 120; deep sleep 86; differing views on importance of induction 101; early learning set induction xii, 36–38, 45, 88, 95; Erickson's view on 132–133; indirect hypnotic induction 5; poetry in 88–89; stages of hypnotic induction 24, 31, 67; waiting technique 68; woman having undergone mastectomy, case example 82–85; *see also* A Guided Fantasy (Sidney Rosen); hypnosis; One Thousand Induction Techniques and Their Application to Therapy and Thinking (Sidney Rosen); time
injunctive approach 118–119
inner search 22–23, 24, 27, 68
"innocent eye" concept 4
insight: vs. experiencing 25; role of in Erickson's thinking 20, 65–66, 124; role of in most psychotherapies 26
interspersed suggestions 28, 117–118, 120

Japanese culture, Bucholtz and Rosen's love for vii
Judaism: Kabbalistic type experience 91; symbols of Kaballa 50
Jung, Carl, collective unconscious 89

Kaballa *see* Judaism
Kamlya, J. 101
Kasson, Martin 112–115
Kiarsis, Victor: friendship with Rosen xi; overview of Rosen's essays on Erickson xi–xiii
Klein, M.H. 19
Knight, Mrs. 17–18
Kubie, Lawrence 20, 33, 72
Kundalini-type experience 91

language: "I know that I can never really understand the language of another person" (Erickson) 20; patient's own language 66, 70; *see also* The Evocative Power of Language (Sidney Rosen); nonverbal communication
learning: doing and learning 8–10; learning- rather than pathology-focused approach 21; *see also* unconscious learnings
Leuner, Hanscarl 100
limitations 1–2, 6, 16, 17, 28; unconscious self-limitations 45
"living poetic" concept viii–ix
logotherapy 113
Longfellow, Henry Wadsworth, "Into each life some rain must fall" 9, 80
Lowen, Reich 114

McCue, E.C. 49
McCue, P.A. 49
magic: childhood as world of magic viii–ix, 21–22, 92, 96; magical protection by touching objects 50
manipulation 2, 10, 76, 125, 134; influencing patients (inevitable and helpful) 108–109; *see also* Concretizing of Symptoms and Their Manipulation (Sidney Rosen)
mantras 35, 36
marathon group therapy 113, 114
marijuana: Erickson's views on 13; vs. hypnotic intervention in cancer cases 78
marriage, Erickson's views on 12
Maslow, Abraham 113

mastery, sense of 10, 16, 25, 28, 68, 77, 78, 80
Mead, Margaret 65, 66, 124, 128, 131
meditation 32, 35, 64
mediumship 65
memory: early memory experiencing 25; Erikson on 6; and experiencing 97, 98; *see also* corrective regression
Mental Research Institute (Palo Alto) 64
Mesmer, Franz 38, 63
metaphors 67, 117, 118, 119, 132, 137; metaphorical responses from Erickson 124; metaphorical suggestions 81; "smorgasbord" metaphor 29; *see also* "mountain" metaphor
Mill, John Stuart 48
mindfulness 2; *see also* experiencing
Mintz, Elizabeth 114
Minuchin, Salvador 14, 21
modeling and role-modeling 16, 20, 42, 67, 135–136
Moreno, Jacob Levy 115
"mountain" metaphor: "I like to climb a mountain" (Erickson) 5, 63, 127; "I like to climb a mountain" (Rosen) 89, 91–92, 95; "Therapy is like a snowball rolling down a mountain" (Erickson) 23, 75, 128
multilevel communication 21

nausea, anticipatory 81
neo-Freudians 66
New Age healing approaches 35
New York Milton H. Erickson Society for Hypnosis and Psychotherapy (NYSEPH) vii, xi
nonverbal communication 20, 67, 72
nonverbal suggestions 36, 63
novelty 16, 19

objects *see* physical objects
Occam's Razor 8
One Thousand Induction Techniques and Their Application to Therapy and Thinking (Sidney Rosen): chapter overview by Kiarsis xii; early learning set induction 36–38, 45; first conscious then automatic 39–41; focusing and trance state 31–36, 41, 45, 46; "hurt feelings state" example 40–41; imagination and imagery 32, 38; indirect suggestion and utilization approach 31; stages of hypnotic induction 31; substituting good

ideas for bad ones 32, 38, 41; switching technique 32, 38–39, 40, 42, 43; thinking 42–46; thinking about what to do next, steps for 44–45; thinking big 45; trance in psychotherapy 41–42; *see also* A Guided Fantasy (Sidney Rosen); hypnosis; induction techniques; trance state
optical illusions 46
optimism 1, 2, 3–4, 16, 17, 28
Oracle of Delphi 23
oracular pronouncements, interpretations and directions 22–23
Orne, M. 36, 100–101

pain: cancer patients 77, 78, 86; case of patient with abdominal pain 47, 53–54; and concretizing of symptoms 48–49, 51, 52; elevating the pain 75; Erickson on 2, 9; feeling the patient's pain 72; and imagination 38; relief from vs. achieving one's potential 16, 17; and switches 39, 64; temporomandibular pain (Kay Thompson) 119; transferred to clenched fist (Kay Thompson) 117, 119; and willpower 32
Palo Alto, Mental Research Institute 64
panic 38, 39, 52; panic attack 52
Paracelsus 27, 32, 38
"paradoxical intention" concept 104
parapsychology 2, 7
patient: autosuggestions 8, 26–27, 73, 101; "First you model the patient's world, and then you role model the patient's world" (Erickson) 16, 20, 42, 67, 135, 136; influencing patients (inevitable and helpful) 108–109; "It is the patient who does the work" (Erickson) ix, 123, 124; patient's goals 129, 134; patient's own language 66, 70; patient's responsibilities and involvement in planning treatment 109–110, 112; protection of patient 5–6; therapist-patient relationship 24; using patients' values to change their attitudes 81–82; what is patient cured from/to 28, 112
patients' stories: actress with multiple sclerosis (Louise) 104–105; the "African violet queen of Milwaukee" 9; college freshman wanting to quit school 73–75; "I'm going to die next Saturday morning" story 27; man with compulsion to visit restrooms 98–99; patient with abdominal pain 47, 53–54; patient with fear of heights and allergies 47, 56–58; patient with fear of swimming and self-condemnation (*The February Man*) 122, 123, 124, 125, 126; patient with hair-pulling compulsion (trichotillomania) 47, 54–56; patient with nausea as result of chemotherapy 58–60; Sara (ex-nun), case of 47, 51; woman having undergone mastectomy 82–85; woman seeing "LOVE" broken in two 51; woman with agoraphobic symptoms 73; woman with breast cancer 79–80; woman with hallucinations of naked men 48–49; woman with large gap between front teeth 71
Pavlov, Ivan 113
Pecci, Ernest F. 7
Perls, Fritz S. 101, 102, 103–104, 106, 109, 112, 113
personality types 3
Pesso, Albert 115
phobias 25, 38, 39, 51, 73; phobic desensitization 113; *see also* agoraphobia; desensitization; fear of height; hair-pulling compulsion (trichotillomania)
physical objects: concretizing of 49–50, 52; magical protection of 50
Pierrakos, John 114
poetry: Emerson on ix; in Erickson's hypnotic inductions 88–89; in Erickson's post-hypnotic suggestions 13; Kay Thompson's poetic language 119; "living poetic" concept viii–ix; poetic elements of psyche 137; and therapeutic healing vii–viii
Portnoy, Isidore 72
post-hypnotic suggestions 13, 39, 68, 117, 119, 120; indirect post-hypnotic suggestions 129, 132
presentness 101, 102
privacy 6
"projection into future" technique 78–79; example of woman with breast cancer 79–80
projections *see* externalizations
protection of patient 5–6
pseudo-explanations, vs. explanations 26
psychoanalysis/psychoanalytic therapies: comparison with Erickson's approach 75, 131; early memory experiencing 25; focusing and trance state 35; free association 27; insight vs. trance state

65–66; non-directive techniques 100; positive transference 27; as slower form of hypnotic therapy 27; suggestion 26, 27; therapeutic modalities 113; therapist's degree of involvement 19; touching involvements 114; trance in 41; "value-free" issue 2, 109; *see also* Freud, Sigmund; Horney, Karen; Jung, Carl
psychodrama 115
psychological approaches, historical perspective 113–115
psycho-motor therapy 115
psychosomatic responses 39
The Psychotherapeutic and Hypnotherapeutic Approaches of Milton H. Erickson (Sidney Rosen): chapter overview by Kiarsis xii; contribution to anthropology 65; contribution to family therapy 64–65; "Dry Beds" story 63–64, 68–76; empirical approach 66; first international Erickson congress (1980) 64–65, 67; "First you model the patient's world, and then you role model the patient's world" 67; "Hypnosis is the evocation and utilization of unconscious learnings" 66; "I like to climb a mountain" 63; patient's own language and the nonverbal 66–67; reframing 66; Rosen's friends' (Jack and Art) meeting with Erickson 62–63, 67; Rosen's introduction to hypnosis 62; Rosen's meetings with Erickson 63, 67; Rosen's writings on Erickson's work 67; stages of hypnotic induction and interruption of usual mental set 67–68; suggestions, inclusion of in trance 66; suggestions, post-hypnotic 68; suggestions and unconscious mind 63; switches 64; trance state vs. insight 65–66; *see also* "Dry Beds" story
puzzles 45, 46

racial and genetic differences, Erickson's views on 12–13
realism 1–2, 16, 17
reassurance (or "real-assurance") 52
Recent Experiences with Gestalt, Encounter and Hypnotic Techniques (Sidney Rosen): article published after first meeting with Erickson 67, 97; chapter overview by Kiarsis xiii; dangers of encounter groups 111; dream interpretation (Gestalt) 106–107; Encounter therapy 97, 100, 107–108, 111; experiencing (not talking about) 109; experiencing, re-experiencing, and corrective experiences 97–98; Gestalt therapy 97–98, 101–107, 109, 111, 113, 134; health or flight into health (man with compulsion to visit restrooms) 98–99; hypnosis, experiments on nature of 100–101; hypnosis, innovative techniques 100; hypnotic experiences in Encounter and Gestalt groups 107–108; influencing patients (inevitable and helpful) 108–109; Martin Kasson's discussion of Rosen's paper 112–115; patient's responsibilities and involvement in planning treatment 109–110, 112; physical encounters (Louise case) 104–105; presentness 101, 102; taking back externalizations 103–104; therapist's and patient's roles 111–112; What am I being cured to as well as what am I being cured of? 112; *see also* Encounter therapy; Gestalt therapy
reframing: and anxiety 17; central part of Ericksonian therapy 18, 20, 66; and corrective regression 122, 123, 125; examples of reframing 71, 73, 82, 125; Kay Thompson's use of reframing 117, 119; positive reframing 26
Reich, Wilhelm 114
Relaxation Response 35
relaxation therapies 42
religion 2, 8, 50, 64
resistance 28, 62, 71
Rhine, J.B. 7
Richeport, Madeleine 65
ritual trance 65
Rogers, Carl 113
role-modeling 16, 20, 42, 67, 135–136
Rosen, Sidney: Bucholtz, meeting with vii; Bucholtz on his essays on Erickson viii–x; Erickson, meetings with 63, 67, 97, 133; Erickson's choice of Rosen and Rossi to present his theories 128, 130; Erickson's hypnosis of Rosen (tendency to intellectualize) 123, 127; Erickson's invitation to write foreword to *Hypnotherapy: An Exploratory Casebook* (Erickson and Rossi) 67; his friends' (Jack and Art) meeting with Erickson 62–63, 67; hypnosis, introduction to 62; Japanese culture, love for shared with

Bucholtz vii; Kiarsis, friendship with xi; Kiarsis on his essays on Erickson xi–xiii; *My Voice Will Go with You: The Teaching Tales of Milton H. Erickson, M.D.* (Erickson and Rosen) xi, xii, xiii, 6, 67, 128, 135, 136; NYSEPH founding president xi; photographs of xv, xvi, xvii; professional activity and school of psychotherapy xi, 130; writings on Erickson's work 67; *see also essay titles*
Rossi, Ernest L.: on depotentiation of usual mental sets 24, 67, 133; on Erickson's atheoretical approach 134; Erickson's choice of Rosen and Rossi to present his theories 128, 130; *Hypnotherapy: An Exploratory Casebook* (Erickson and Rossi) 31, 41, 67, 123–124, 125–126, 127, 130; on hypnotic induction stages 24, 31, 67; *Hypnotic Realities* (Erickson and Rossi) 130, 131–132, 134; on inner search 68; photograph of xvii; professional activity and school of psychotherapy 130
"roughage of life" (Erickson) 93
Rubin, Alex 115
Rusk Institute for Rehabilitation Medicine (New York) 63

Sacerdote, Pearl: guided hypnotic dreams 100; Hallucinated Sensory Hypnoplasty 100
Schutz, Will 114
Sector, I.I., *The Practical Applications of Medical and Dental Hypnosis* (Erickson, Hershman, and Sector) 130
self-acceptance 104
self-concept, change of 24–25
self-hypnosis: and cancer patients 78, 80, 81, 85; and control of entry into states of mind 39; and "hurt feelings state" 40; and power of imagination 32; and sense of mastery 25; therapists' use of 72, 87; vs. trance state 33
self-suggestions 36
sensory hypnoplasty 100
Shakespeare, William, Hamlet's soliloquy 29
shamans 32, 38, 50; *see also* healers
shiatsu 35
Shin Buddhist group (Japan), statues and religious objects 50
Shinto religion, animal symbols 50
Simonton, O.C. 80

Simonton, S. 80
Skinner, B.F. 113
smoking habit 52, 93
"smorgasbord" metaphor 29
solution-oriented therapies 41–42
Speak to the wall so the door may hear (Sufi saying) 130
"start and stop" technique 71, 119
Stevens, J. 50
Stevens, L.S. 50
Stories for the Third Ear Foreword (Sidney Rosen): chapter overview by Kiarsis xiii; modeling and role-modeling 135–136; teaching tales (Erickson) 135, 136, 137; teaching tales (Lee Wallas) 136–137; unconscious learnings 136–137
storytelling 42, 68, 117, 119, 128, 135; *see also* teaching tales
subvocal speech 7
Sufi: preparation and imparting of teaching 137; Speak to the wall so the door may hear (saying) 130; stories 68
suggestions: autosuggestions 8, 26–27, 73, 101; compound suggestions 129, 132; direct suggestions 75, 128, 133; ego-boosting suggestions 25; ego-syntonic suggestions 36, 72; heterosuggestions 26, 27–28, 101; hypersuggestibility 33, 73; and imagination 63–64; indirect suggestions 28, 31, 65, 73, 81, 125; in induction of trance 66; interspersed suggestions 28, 117–118, 120; metaphorical suggestions 81; nonverbal suggestions 36, 63; post-hypnotic suggestions 39, 68, 117, 119, 120; post-hypnotic suggestions, indirect 129, 132; in psychoanalysis 26, 27; self-suggestions 36; and unconscious mind 36, 63
superego 11, 103
supernatural 7–8
switching technique/switches 32, 38–39, 40, 42, 43, 53, 64, 77
symbols: concretizing of 47; concretizing vs. symbolizing 50–52; in religions and healing practices 50
sympathetic identification 86–87
symptoms: "prescribing the symptom" (Jay Haley) 126; *see also* Concretizing of Symptoms and Their Manipulation (Sidney Rosen)

Tantric practices 35
teaching tales 42, 135, 136–137; *see also* storytelling
"teaching trance" ("therapizing") 120
temporomandibular pain, Kay Thompson's treatment of 119
therapeutic double bind approach 129, 132
therapies, historical perspective 113–115
therapist: goals of 16, 28; heterosuggestions 26, 27–28, 101; influencing patients (inevitable and helpful) 108–109; role of according to Erickson 19–20, 75–76; role of according to Rosen 111–112; self-hypnosis 72; sympathetic identification 86–87; therapist-patient relationship 24; *see also* manipulation
"therapizing" ("teaching trance") 120
thinking: and induction techniques 42–46; steps for thinking what to do next 44–45; thinking big 45
Thompson, Kay *see* The Evocative Power of Language (Sidney Rosen)
time: "projection into future" technique 78–80; time distortion techniques 80–81, 82, 86, 118, 120, 129, 132; time progression 101; time regression 98
"top dog" - "underdog" inner dialogue 103
Topsys and Turvys (book) 45–46
trance state: deep vs. common everyday trance 129, 132; and ego-syntonic suggestions 72; group trance 88, 97; induction of and suggestions 66; vs. insight 65–66; intense interpersonal trances 118; nature of 31–36; in psychotherapy 41–42; ritual trance 65; therapeutic trance state 73; "therapizing/ teaching trance" 120; and trance state 24; from trance to trance 120; and unconscious mind 24, 56, 88, 90–91; as unique state of awareness and receptivity 101; *see also* A Guided Fantasy (Sidney Rosen); hypnosis; One Thousand Induction Techniques and Their Application to Therapy and Thinking (Sidney Rosen)
tranquilizers 23–24
transactional analysis 115
transference 20; positive transference 27
trichotillomania (hair-pulling compulsion), case of patient with 47, 54–56

unconscious: Erickson's view of 22, 89; Freud's theory of 89; Jung's collective unconscious 89; unconscious self-limitations 45; wisdom of 4–5, 6, 129, 132; *see also* unconscious learnings; unconscious mind
unconscious learnings: and cancer patients 77, 83; and concretizing of resources 53; and conscious minds 129; and corrected experience 98; *A Guided Fantasy* example 88, 89, 90–91; "Hypnosis is the evocation and utilization of unconscious learnings" (Erickson) 16, 20, 23, 27, 33, 66, 75, 136; *see also* unconscious; unconscious mind
unconscious mind: and cancer patients 80, 83; and hypnosis 24, 27, 33; literalness of 60; and problem solving 42; as protector of conscious mind 5, 22; and suggestions 36, 63; and thinking 42–45; and trance state 24, 56, 88, 90–91; trust in 4–5, 71, 120; *see also* unconscious; unconscious learnings
uniqueness (of the individual) 1, 3
utilization approach 31, 129, 132

The Values and Philosophy of Milton H. Erickson (Sidney Rosen): chapter overview by Kiarsis xi–xii; death 14; dreams 2; esthetics 13; experiencing 5; humor 2, 14; imagination 5; learning and doing 8–10; limitations and assets 1–2, 6; manipulation 2, 10; marijuana 13; marriage 12; mindfulness 2; optimism 1, 2, 3–4; protection of patient 5–6; racial and genetic differences 12–13; raising children 10–12; realism 1–2; religion 2, 8; supernatural and ESP 7–8; unconscious, wisdom of 4–5, 6; uniqueness of individual 1, 3; women, attitudes to 12

waiting technique 68
Wallas, Lee *see* Stories for the Third Ear Foreword (Sidney Rosen)
water, as concretizing resource 52, 53
Watts, Alan 113
Watzlawick, Paul 25–26, 65, 66
welfare aid, Erickson's views on 9–10
Wenkart, Antonia 104
What Makes Ericksonian Therapy So Effective? (Sidney Rosen): chapter

overview by Kiarsis xii; consciousness, altered states of (interpersonally) 24; consciousness, altered states of (intrapsychically) 23–24; corrective regression 20; defining Ericksonian therapy 18; encouraging minimal change 16–17, 23; experience counts 25–26; explanations and pseudo-explanations 26; flexibility and adaptability 20; gurus, healers, and therapists 17–18; humor 16, 28–29; learning- rather than pathology-focused approach 21; magic and entering new reality 21–22; multilevel communication 21; novelty 16, 19; optimism 16, 17, 28; oracular pronouncements, interpretations and directions 22–23; reframing 17, 18, 20; self-concept, change of 24–25; smorgasbord metaphor 29; suggestion (autosuggestions) 26–27; suggestions (heterosuggestions) 26, 27–28; therapist activity 19–20; therapist's goals 16, 28; unconscious learnings 16; what is patient cured from/to 28; "When a person entered into Erickson's sphere" paragraph viii–ix, 21

Whitehorn, J.C. 19
Wiesel, Elie, on writing 43
willpower, and imagination 32
witch doctors 50
Wolpe, Joseph 113
women, Erickson's views on 12
word play 28, 117, 118, 119, 120
writers block 64, 71, 74–75
writing, Elie Wiesel on 43

yantras 35
Yeats, W. B. 5; *The Lake Isle of Innisfree* 13

Zeig, J.K., *A Teaching Seminar with Milton H. Erickson* 12, 28, 71
Zen stories 68
zone therapy 35

CPSIA information can be obtained
at www.ICGtesting.com
Printed in the USA
BVHW062128020320
573873BV00012B/143